Walk
With
Me

1-26-2010

Edited by Peggy Mercer.

First printing, December 2009.

ISBN-13: 978-0-9822189-8-3
ISBN-10: 0-9822189-8-2

Cover design by Debbie Lankford and ThomasMax (Lee Clevenger & R. Preston Ward)

Cover photo credits: *Douglas Enterprise* and the Douglas Regional Airport for the pictures of J.D. and the flags. National Archives Records Administration for the Lone soldier walking in the woods.

Photos of the Stalag IXB Prison Barracks and the Celebrating Freedom at Stalag IXB also courtesy of National Archives Records Administration.

Published by:

 tm

ThomasMax Publishing
P.O. Box 250054
Atlanta, GA 30325
404-794-6588
www.thomasmax.com

Walk With Me

by J.D. Lankford

ThomasMax

Your Publisher
For The 21st Century

Editor's Note

Walking with retired United States Army SFC J.D. Lankford, writer and WWII hero, through these war stories and vignettes of his growing up has been a mesmerizing experience. It is not often I come across a story so powerful and historically significant. A story so memorable I will never forget it. As I edited this great book, sometimes I laughed and sometimes I cried. And sometimes I felt a cold chill.

The story you hold in your hands it not for the faint-hearted. It reminds each of us that freedom is not free and that our daily lives are blessed because of great American heroes like J.D. Lankford, who thank God, walked this soldier's road before us.

Peggy Mercer
Award winning author of the children's book, *There Come a Soldier*,
Handprint Books,
New York, 2007

Introduction

If you want to know something about the Great Depression of the 1930's, Walk With Me.

If you want to know about the 1933 Tree Army, stated by President Franklin Delano Roosevelt, which took over three million young men, gave them jobs when one of every four persons was out of work, and creating the Civilian Conservation Corps, "C.C.C" at a dollar a day wages, Walk With Me.

Walk With Me through my Military Service. If you want to know, how wars are fought, then let's get down to where the rubber meets the road in battle.

Walk With Me as a Prisoner of War, (P.O.W.) in a Nazi prison camp in Germany. Where every human right was stripped from me and I was forced to live like an animal trying to survive on one loaf of black bread divided among twelve men for one day's rations. I weighed 188 pounds when captured. Six months later, when I was liberated, my weight was 93 pounds.

Walk With Me as I came home to Georgia, got married, and then after a while returned to duty.

Walk With Me. To Korea and again into battle. I already had four Bronze Battle Stars and received five more Bronze Battle Stars for services in Korea.

Walk With Me. In Korea and then, on returning back to the States for stateside duty.

Walk with Me as I took my family back to Germany on a three year hitch. During that time in Germany, the wife and boys wanted to visit the prison camp I had been in. You will see the pictures we took.

Walk With Me, as I then returned from Germany to duty in the United States until I retired.

I invite you to walk with me now through the pages of my life.

J. D. Lankford
Author

*This book is lovingly dedicated to my wife Debbie
with all my love and heartfelt appreciation.
She has patience and understanding. She is my anchor who
understands me better than anyone else and still loves me!*

My daughter Christine, whom I love and cherish very much.

My grandchildren, Marshall, Amber, Sara, Noah and David

*My great grandchildren, (present and future):
Cody and Cole Knight, Hunter Lankford and Adam Hamilton, who
made his appearance on Veteran's Day, November 11, 2009. My hope
is that they know and realize that freedom isn't free.*

*That men and women put their lives on the line and fought for their
country, and some were held captive as Prisoners of War.*

*There were many that paid the ultimate price
and didn't make it home.*

*"Freedom isn't free."
Pa Pa D" was very Blessed that he made it home.*

In Loving Memory:

Mildred, Ronald and Donald Lankford

My father and mother, (James Daniel Lankford and Iris Joyce), were married January 9, 1916. By July 1934 they had nine children, six boys and three girls: Buford, Hubert, Lucy, J.D., W.T. (Bill), W. C. (Chester), Faye, Ida Mae, and Raymond.

My oldest brother, Buford was only 12 years old when the stock market crashed. I was six years old and by 1933 when things really got bad, I was just a 10 year old lad trying to survive.

You talk about hard times. Oh, Brother! If you weren't there no way you could understand just how bad things were. My father was a sharecropper. The more children you had the better chance in being accepted by a Farmer to work with you on a share crop basis. The more children, the more work force. My father made a trade with a farmer, a Mr. Jake Vickers, who owned a large farm out on the Hebron Church area a few miles northwest of Douglas, Georgia in Coffee County, in 1931. We moved there and worked for Mr. Vickers until early 1934.

In 1933 it was so dry all of our wells went dry. The only water we could get was from the Satilla River by Hebron Church. My father would hitch-up the team to the wagon, put two large barrels in the wagon and we'd go to the river for water. My father would go down to the water and fill two large buckets, carry them up to the wagon and place them on the back of the wagon.

Bill and I would empty the water buckets into the barrels. After the barrels were filled, we'd tied burlap bags over the top of the barrels so the water would not spill. We used that water for everything. One morning, we had just got back with the water and went to the tobacco beds to pull weeds. Back then when tobacco plants came up, weeds came up too. The only way to remove them was by hand. A tobacco bed was about ten feet wide and about fifty feet long, depending on your need. The framework around the beds was constructed mainly of logs, reason being, when pulling weeds and grass you had to lay a long board across the beds to sit or lay on. This enabled you to get to the weeds in the middle of the beds. You could not walk for damaging the young plants.

To remove the weeds and grass without damaging the young plants, we used a peg constructed of a small flat piece of wood about the size of a Popsicle stick. With one end shaped like a flat blade screw driver, holding the peg between your thumb and forefinger, we pushed the peg into the ground beside the weed or grass. Then using our thumb we used the peg so as not to disturb the young plants.

One day, my mother went to the house to fix lunch. She had been gone maybe half an hour when she began screaming. It was a short distance to the house, so my father jumped on the mule and headed for the house. The house was on fire, burning around the kitchen stove flue. Everything was so dry, some of the sparks had fallen onto the shingle roof.

As I look back, I thank God for the blessings he bestowed upon us that day. We would have lost our house and everything we had, had we not gotten up before day, gone to Hebron and gotten those two barrels of water. By then the fire was out the water was gone. Back to the lake again.

My father started farming with Mr. Vickers the first year with a $300.00 loan. The crops were so bad we were forced to farm with Mr. Vickers a couple more years before we broke even. In 1935 the Government helped my father lease a farm in a place known as Downing, Georgia located about six miles southeast of Douglas. At the time I was 12 years old. I'm not sure just how the deal came about, but the Government not only helped with the leasing, but we were also provided with a mule, equipment, and farm supplies.

Our church provided us with shoes and clothing. The government helped with commodities such as canned beef, dried milk, flour, meal and dried fruits.

The first year on the Downing, Georgia farm was rough going.

When Franklin Delano Roosevelt accepted the Democratic Presidential nomination in 1932, he made a statement which was to change forever the politics of the United States. He said, "I pledge you, I pledge myself, to a new deal for the American people".

When he took office on March 4, 1933, 12 to 15 million people, or one worker out of every four were out of work.

To keep the pledge, he made, President Roosevelt called congress into special session on March 5, 1933. Their purpose was to work on emergency bills. They produced much legislation, many agencies and programs made famous by initials, NRA (National Recovery Administration), FDIC (Federal Deposit Insurance Corporation), AAA (Agricultural Adjustment Administration), PWA (Public Works Administration), HOLC (Home Owners Loan Corporation), TVA (Tennessee Valley Authority), FAC (Farm Credit Administration), and CCC (Civilian Conservation Corps).

The WPA provided projects to help the needy. My father was given a job working for the WPA. My two older brothers farmed along with the rest of the family. The only bad thing about my father's job was that it was over six miles to Douglas and we had no kind of transportation except one mule, and she was needed on the farm. My father would get up early to walk to Douglas in time to catch a truck to take him and the rest of the crew to where they worked. At the end of the day, the truck took the crew back to Douglas and my father walked the six miles back home. My father did this for about three years, five days a week. By 1938 we had our own mules and equipment.

My father paid fifteen dollars for a Model T Ford car. He couldn't drive it home so someone else brought it home, for him. No one in the family could drive, except me. And I learned to drive by getting Uncle Bill home on Saturday nights.

It went like this, on Saturday, after lunch Uncle Bill would go to Douglas taking me with him. Yes, he would get drunk. And yes it was my job to get him home. Uncle Bill would make me sit in his lap (for I was so small I could not reach the gas pedal or the clutch.) Uncle Bill did all the gear shifting and smashing the gas pedal. All I had to do was steer. I had to keep Uncle Bill's Dodge truck between the ditches.

So I wound up being the driver of the Model T for our family.

About this time, my father rented a farm from Mr. Mac Jowers of Ambrose, Georgia, so we moved again. This farm was located between Ambrose and Broxton. It was a large farm. My father's first cousin, Richard Jewell and his family rented half of the farm and we rented the other half. In those days such a farm was considered a two horse farm.

On moving day to the Jowers place, all preparations were made. The pigs and chickens were ready for their cages and the wagon was loaded. Everything seemed to be in order but, when the word *but* comes up, the whole situation changes.

Now my older brother, Buford had joined the CCC and was in camp in Fargo, Georgia. Hubert, the next oldest brother, had been struck by a car while crossing the road a couple years prior. He had received head and other injuries which he never recovered from. In fact part of Hubert's brain died. He just wasn't Hubert after that.

My brother Bill was not quite old enough to go with Hubert on the wagon loaded with all the household goods. It would take from four to five hours to make the trip and Hubert was not capable of making it by himself. I loaded everyone except Hubert in the old Model T and left early. I wanted to get my father to Douglas in time to catch the work truck.

I took the rest of the family to the new place. When I returned to get Hubert and the wagon, Hubert had loaded the chicken crate on the very top of the loaded wagon. Now Hubert had made the crate and he was real proud of the crate. I should have checked it but I didn't which proved to be a mistake.

With a chain Hubert and I hooked the car to the back of the wagon and were on our way. Earlier, my father and I had planned our route. We were to keep out of downtown Douglas as much as possible.

Well things didn't go exactly as we had planned. We encountered our first problem when we reached the intersection of Axson Road and Bowens Mill Road. Things began to happen. Now years later when prior to the move we had gotten another mule. He was a small white mule, (only the Lord knows what would have happened if he had been a large mule). We had quite a time with getting him to work with old Beck the other mule.

This mule was the meanest, most hard headed thing I had ever seen. When I tied the ham string, he bit me. Hooked the trace chains, he kicked me. Given a chance, he pawed me. Ride him? Forget about that. He reminded me of a joke. It was said this man advertised he specialized in training mules. A man took a mule to him for training. After telling the trainer how the mule acted, the trainer took the mule behind the barn. He reached down and picked up a piece of 2x4 about 6 feet long, struck the mule behind the ears with a swift blow and down went the mule. The man was furious, wanting to know why the trainer had killed his mule.

"Oh, he's not dead," explained the trainer. "You see before you can teach a mule anything, you have to get his attention first."

I had long ago given up on ever getting him to settle down, and years when we traded him he was still mean!

Back to the trip. At the intersection we waited for a truck to go by. The Model T truck was pulling farm equipment behind and of course "Buddy" the mule, got spooked. You talk about showing out? He did his part and then some! If Beck, the other mule had not remained calm I don't know what would have happened. Also, to consider, is that about half a mile prior reaching the intersection, Hubert got tired of sitting where he was and decided to move. He got up on top of the chicken crate which already extended about four feet above the wagon body.

Well at the intersection, when Buddy put on his act, things began to happen fast. Buddy bucked, kicked, snorted and tried to launch forward but Beck held her ground.

Hubert picked up his little dog, held him in his lap, and held on. Pretty soon, the chicken crate with Hubert and the dog on it shot forward and broke apart. The chickens flew and ran in all directions. Hubert landed on the tongue of the wagon. Sadly, Hubert's little dog was run over by the wagon.

Buddy continued to buck and kick with both hind feet. Only a miracle saved Hubert from being killed or seriously injured. When I finally got Hubert back into the wagon I was able to get to Buddy's head by following the lines. After a bit, he settled down, not before household items were strung all over the road. Dog dead, no chickens in sight, but the pigs were safe in the base of the wagon.

We finally got all the items back on the wagon and made our way around Douglas. We came out to the Ocilla highway by the farmers market at the Rocky Pond road which took us to the Broxton-Ambrose road. After a couple of hours we reached the junction of the Broxton-Ambrose road.

After turning left at the junction going toward Ambrose, about half a mile up the road was a bridge. Buddy didn't want to cross over the bridge so we went another round with him.

From the looks of things, Buddy wasn't the only mule that didn't like bridges. There was a wagon trail running along the side of the bridge where mules and wagons forded the creek instead of crossing the bridge. We were a little over a mile away and I was eager to get Hubert and the wagon home so I could take old Tin Lizzie and pick up my father after work. I didn't want to be after dark doing so. The lights on the old Model T were so bad, you had to strike a match to see if they were burning.

At this bridge Buddy won. We forded the creek and finally reached home. I made it back to Douglas, picked up Dad and made it to within sight of the house when old Tine Lizzie decided she'd had enough for today. I opened the door and stepped out, saying, "So have I old girl." And we walked to the house. Next morning was Saturday, so Dad didn't have to go to work. While eating breakfast, my Mom looked at me and said, "When was the last time you put gas in old Lizzie?"

"I don't know," I answered

"You might want to check it," she said and I did. Sure enough, it was out of gas.

We got settled in our new house and things seemed to be going well. My father continued working with the WPA. He made a deal to go back and forth to work with the man who carried Mr. Jewell and other from our area. That left me and Hubert to do the farming. Bill, two years younger than me, soon replaced Hubert as my helper. Hubert could (and would) do a good job as long as someone told him what to do and how. After Bill started helping out I was able to go to school. At least twice a week most of the time. I was almost18 years old and had only completed the sixth grade.

I knew I had to get some education. My father as far as I knew had never gone to school. He could not write his name, had no kind of trade whatsoever to take him from behind a pair of plow handles or a shovel. All he ever knew was manual labor. I would never settle for that.

So, let me say here, while I don't have a masters or PhD, when my schooling stopped I had two years of college in business administration. It's not very, much but at least I can write my name!

One Saturday morning, Dad and I looked over what progress had been made that week in the fields. Dad stopped walking, turned to me and asked, "J.D., what's on your mind?"

"Show's huh?" I said.

"Very much. You want to tell me?" Said Dad.

"Not really," I said. "It seems I have no choice. I really think you don't realize the position you are asking me to fill."

"Oh yes I do. I regret having to do so, but when you are between the hard place and a rock, things don't always work out as you'd have them too. So before you say anymore let me have my say, and if you want to talk, then I'll listen. I have an idea that might be what we're both looking for. First I'm needed here on the farm. I know what you face each day. I also know you understand the money I make on the job is needed to help the family survive.

"If we had another income to offset at least some of what I make we could make it pretty good until the crops come in. I would be glad to swap a shovel handle for a set of plow handles any day." He Stopped talking and stared at the field's, then added, I also know as long as you are on this farm you will not be able to go to school like you should."

Dad put his hand on my shoulder; I don't want you to grow up having to find whatever work you can get to live on for the lack of education. "I want you to consider this carefully. Your brother tells me where he's at in the CCC they have an education department. One can go to school and get an education. I know you want to go to school and I've thought a great deal about this lately. If you were to join the CCC, first your income to the family would offset some of what I make. Second you could get some education. Third, I can return to the farm. If you think it's the thing to do go for it. If not, start talking and let's see what we can come up with."

I said, "Dad, look at me. I'm almost 18 years old and I doubt if I weigh a 100 pounds, and yes I've given much thought to the idea, but I have no knowledge what the requirements are."

"Have you tried to find out?"

"No, sir." I said.

"Well why not fill out an application and go from there if that's what you want."

"I would almost be willing to do anything to have gone to school."

"The decision is yours."

I took Dad's advice and filled out an application. It seemed forever before I got a letter telling me to report to the CCC Camp in Fargo, Georgia, 65 miles from where I lived. I went right away.

Three others had received letters telling them to report to Camp Fargo, and so several other men were there also. It was 9 o'clock before the Doctor got to camp and started the physicals.

First we had to remove everything except our outer pants and form a line to be weighed. This was as far as I got. The man looked at me and said, "Son, you have to weigh at least 100 pounds to be accepted. You weigh only 98." Then he stopped talking, looked at me for a moment and reached into his pocket. He pulled out a 50 cent piece. He bent over and whispered into my ear and handed the 50 cents to me. "Go down to the store and get all the bananas you can eat son, then come back."

When I got to the store I got ten cents' worth and ate them. I figured I might be able to hold another five cents' worth, so I did.

On returning, the man at the scales looked at me and said, "Son strip everything off but your outer pants and step on the scale as instructed." He adjusted the scale, looked at me and smiled and said, "Next man!"

I handed him the thirty-five cents that was left out of the fifty cents he had given me. He winked and slapped me on the back as I stepped off the scales.

   Little did I know, I would be with, or under complete control of the Military for over the next twenty-three years. It was a complete change in life for me.

   I never knew that unity bonded military personnel so. Learning to cope with the new adventure was no problem for me. I found it to be challenging and exciting! A country boy, never been out of Georgia and only out of Coffee County a very few times, all I knew how to do was follow a mule and plow. One thing about my training I respected most of all, I had someone tell me what to do and how to do it. I didn't have to figure it out by myself.

Tobacco seed bed

Transplanting tobacco plants from seed beds.

Gathering ripe tobacco leaves

J.D. Lankford

Tobacco Barns were used to cure the leaves.

Firing up the tobacco barn. Someone had to keep a check on the temperature and keep the fire going.

Tobacco sales in South Georgia.

Camp life was different from anything I had ever experienced. Being away from home for the first time, having a job I was paid to do, a dollar a day was hardly lavish. Sure helped feed and care for my family. Knowing the twenty-five dollars was needed back home, I had no problem following the standard daily routine of each enrollee.

My medical care began with inoculations against typhoid fever and smallpox. And the CCC Camp Fargo, Georgia had an infirmary to *treat any illness*. You had to take a bath once a week, brush your teeth daily and keep your hair short, your fingernails short and clean, bedding and clothing clean. All leaders, assistant leaders, supervisors and truck drivers, were required to have a first aid certificate. Not until 1940 did enrollee's take first aid training and everyone was required to attend safety classes and training. Prior to safety training the death rate in the CCC's was 2.25 per one thousand. Due to the success in the safety training classes this rate dropped to 1.14 and .90 per thousand.

The CCC camp base pay thirty dollars a month. Leaders got forty-five dollars, and assistant Leaders got thirty-six. The typical daily routine began with reveille at 6:00 a.m. and then breakfast. Seven thirty a.m. was sick call, making beds, policing the grounds and making ready to load on trucks for the trip into the woods, or whatever you were doing. We worked under experienced foremen; on the job training, the first day on the job taught me a lesson I've never forgotten, listen and respect my leader. I was amazed how our leaders took a bunch of greenhorns, stood them in a line, and walked by, looking at each man. I would not say he was inspecting us. It was more like sizing up each man for the job he was expected to do.

After the leader separated us to his satisfaction, he handed out the working tools, assigned jobs according to the physical condition of each man beginning with the strongest down to the last four of us.

He looked at us and said, "you men will be piling and burning brush and trash."

He looked at me and said, "Your job is to keep the fires going."

I could understand why I was selected for the job. I was thin. If I stood sideways in bright sunlight I hardly made a shadow. I had a good case of the *gone tail*. I was breath and britches, but I sure welcomed the job I had been assigned.

I now want us to look at a little history of the CCC, how it came about why it was organized and who ran it. The Civilian Conservation Corps or "CCC" was not an idea of President Roosevelt's. He had been a conservationist for many years and in 1932, as Governor of New York, had put some of the later CCC concepts into practice. As President, he knew something drastic had to be done about unemployment and waste of natural resources.

Over five million young men were unemployed in 1932, as well as a large number of World War I veterans. These men roamed the country looking for work, went on the welfare roles and/or turned to crime.

At the same time, millions of acres of farmland had eroded and were threatened by fire, because of indiscriminate timber harvesting. Recreational opportunities were almost at a standstill for the lack of budget and personnel problems.

Roosevelt's inauguration was March 4, 1933. Two days later he called a meeting of high government officials to create a Civilian Conservation Corps. His plan was to put up to 500,000 unemployed youths to work in forests, parks and range lands. The Army would run the camps. Agriculture and interior would handle the work projects and personnel to manage them and a budget director would provide financial assistance. The Department of Labor would coordinate the selection of enrollees.

On March 21, the president sent a message to the 73rd Congress on the establishment of the CCC organization: He estimated 250,000 men would be given temporary employment by summer if Congress would give him the authority. He got the authority to proceed to establish the CCC. Rather than establish a new bureaucracy, the President used the existing War, Agriculture, Interior and Labor departments.

The organization was first called Emergency Conservation Work, but in the President's congressional speech, he calls it the "CCC". However it was 1937 before Congress made the name official.

Thirty-seven days elapsed between Roosevelt's inauguration and the signing of the first enrollee on April 7, 1933. Henry Rich of Alexandria Virginia was sent to Camp Roosevelt near Luray, Virginia. History tells us a miracle of cooperation among government agencies occurred. Even mobilization during World War I didn't come close to the CCC effort. The initial call was for 250,000 men to be enrolled by July 1, 1933. Supposedly, they were to be unemployed between 18 and 25 years old and unmarried. There to come from families on relief. Men from every part of the country signed up and were sent to every part of the country.

Because of chronic unemployment and soil erosion on Indian reservations, 14,000 Indians were authorized to enroll in the CCC. These men stayed on their reservation and lived at home under the jurisdiction of the Indian affairs. Another group of men who joined the CCC on April 22, 1933, were Local Experienced Men or L.E.M. and were older men experienced in woodcraft. They were hired to supervise the work crews, (The Forest Service, which was responsible for most of the camp projects didn't have the manpower to manage the thousands of men.) On May 11, 1933 a total of 24,000 World War I (men in their 30's and 40's) were enrolled. Due to unrest and unemployment among the veterans, (especially during the Bonus Army trouble of 1932), a partial solution to the problems was the enrollment of veterans in their own conservation camps.

Oh, yes, Bonus Army Trouble of World War I. Let's go back into history a bit, and take a look at the way the World War I veterans were treated in what was known as the "Tombstone Bonus" due them. When the stock market crashed in 1929, and again in 1932, when one of every four Americans were unemployed; it was a good time to cash in on a bonus Congress had already agreed the veterans deserved.

But the veterans were 13 years early and the government was not ready to pay up. In 1924, Congress agreed World War I veterans should receive financial compensation for economic losses suffered while in the military. Many of the politicians opposed the proposal, but a compromise was reached. It was decided the veteran's bonus would not be issued until 1945. Of course the veterans did not agree and called it the "Tombstone Bonus" because many believed they would be dead before they received it.

Well, the great depression changed everything, so veterans sought immediate payment of the bonus. A former Army Sergeant, Walter W. Water, left Portland, Oregon in May 1932, with 250 unemployed veterans to march on Washington to lobby for their bonuses. By July 1932, well over 20,000 men, women and children descended on Washington. Camps sprang up around the city with many camps near the U.S. Capital building. Naturally politicians viewed the veterans as an unruly mob and revolutionary threat.

The stage was set and the kettle of conflict reached the boiling point.

The March of the Bonus Army is a story of veterans and people, nearly lost to American memory. It is about President Herbert Hoover, ordering the eviction of American veterans and their families from their seat of government. It is a story of military leaders and federal troops scattering marchers with a tear gas assault. It is a story youngest Army Chief of Staff in U.S. Army history, General Douglas MacArthur, Major Dwight D. Eisenhower and Major George S. Patton. It is a story of a nation's Army ordered against its veterans.

Army Chief of Staff, General Douglas MacArthur, went far beyond President Hoover's orders to get the military involved, by authorizing an invasion of Calvary, (led by office George S. Patton), infantrymen and tanks. General MacArthur's principal aide, who argued for fewer troops, was Major Dwight Eisenhower.

It is a story of aftermath of conflict and the tragedy of years to follow. It is the foundation upon which the G.I. Bill of rights would rise; a story of a band of veteran's whose defense of freedom and determination to preserve their freedom of all Americans which made our nation strong. On May 11, 1933, twenty-four thousand World War I veterans were selected as leaders of the CCC to teach and train enrollee's. And what a job they did!

The first day in the woods, the leader looked at me and told me to burn trash and keep the fires going. He gave me a sprayer with fuel in it and showed me how to use it before he let me burn on my own. He taught me a lesson I've never forgotten. Our lunch break was from 12 to 12:30. We were loaded back on the trucks at 4:00 to 4:30 p.m. depending. We returned to camp and held the retreat ceremony, which involved lowering the Flag, and heard announcements. Dinner followed and from then on we were on our own until lights out at 10:00 p. m. Until then, we could go to school, read books, and write letters or just plain shoot the breeze. We could go to town as long as we were back in bed by lights out. On weekends we could then stay out until 12:00 p.m. midnight.

The job I had burning trash lasted about three weeks. I spent most of my spare time in the school department studying. One evening at formation the camp commander announced a group of men were being shipped to California. If any of us wanted to go without be appointed we could do so as long as we had over five months left on our enrollment. A troop train was being put together in Jacksonville, Florida. We would be put on the train within two days. The next day a couple of trucks loaded with troops from our camp headed for the train and I was one of them.

When we got to Jacksonville, we loaded on the troop train. We remained sitting there for another two days waiting for the train to be complete. We finally left the station and I lost knowledge of all time. This old country boy stepped out into another world completely different from anything I had ever known. And the trip to California was something else; it was the first time I had ever been on a train. This was enough to grab your attention within itself.

Sometimes the train was delayed a day at a time in some station without moving, and most of the time church groups and other organizations came by bringing carts of fruit, cookies, candy, drinks and books. I had never received so much at any one time in all my Life! Just being able to have three good meals a day, eating all you wanted without wondering when the next meal would be!

I'm not sure how long it took to get from Jacksonville, Florida to Gilroy, California on the troop train, but it must have been well over two weeks. Each morning they let us off for exercise. Finally we arrived on a Thursday. Trucks were waiting for us, I'm not sure the number of men that arrived at camp #450, I do know that the camp was almost empty.

The camp commander and all the leaders welcomed us. We had until Monday to get settled in. Most of us were under weight and under nourished. History tells us, the CCC men after being in the CCC their first three to four months gained an average of over 11 pounds. Health and safety were of primary importance. The Army was in charge of the health facilities. Each camp had the services of either a medical officer or a contract physician. One morning, I went on sick call with a tooth hurting. In less than an hour I was on my way to downtown Gilroy to a local Dentist. We waited in a small room. Very shortly the Dr. came in pushing a contraption like a large spinning wheel. Attached to the frame was a pole about six feet high. On the other end was a small wheel with lines running from the small wheel to the large wheel on the frame, with a small pulley attached as guides.

The Dr. sat me in another chair and pulled his contraption up. He sat down by me and asked, "Got tooth problems huh?"

All I could do was moan.

I recognized the thing as a dental drill. It was powered by a foot pedal like an old pedal sewing machine. It was the first and last foot powered dental drill I have ever seen. The work he did on my tooth lasted for years.

CCC Camp life we followed a regimented daily routine. No longer were we roaming the streets of our hometowns, or the backwoods or riding the rails in search of work. We had work for which we were thankful and got paid, even though it was only one dollar a day. We gained knowledge and learned.

We ate well and also had the food and medical care we so needed. It's no wonder we gained over eleven pounds in three to four months.

Yes, life in the CCC was different but you could never buy what we learned.

Let me share just a few things the CCC men did by respect, working as a team. Between 1933 to 1942, we laid some 89,000 miles of telephone lines. We developed fire lookout towers and built over three thousand. Fire breaks over an area of 65,000 miles. We developed Public campgrounds on over 50,000 acres, which included 13,000 miles of foot trails. We restored nearly 4,000 historic structures. Planted more than two billion trees.

Originally, CCC projects were confined to forestry, park

development, and soil erosion control, but later included disaster relief, historical restoration and national defense and fighting forest fires. The CCC men spent more than six million man days fighting forest fires.

Back in 1862 when the U.S. Department of Agriculture was founded, it was responsible for agriculture policy and administration of the national forest control. Well, it changed because in 1905, when the U.S. Forest Service was established, it began administering national forest reserves throughout the country. With primary responsibilities being the protection of timber management in the 1930's, there were 150 national forests services located in 39 states as well as Alaska, and Puerto Rico.

The CCC camps located on national, state and private land was controlled by the forest service. The forest service controlled the CCC camps on national forest lands, while the War department controlled the other camps. We went when needed and served.

Fighting fires by CCC men was two-fold. With the vast manpower available from the CCC Corp, trained people manned the fire lines along with regular forest service personnel. The other aspect was fire prevention. We built firebreaks, roads, fire lookouts and airfields, cleared debris and patrolled forest areas. What amazed me was the training required before we were allowed to go near a fire. But being well trained in a job doesn't always provide you with the protection needed. In fact, in August 1937, ten CCC men were lost fighting the black water fire on the Shoshone National Forest in Wyoming.

During the nine years the CCC Corp existed, a total twenty-nine 29 CCC men lost their lives fighting fires. When the CCC organization was established by President Roosevelt, not only did he give jobs to over three million young men over the nine years, but countless jobs went to other people as well. Just a few examples: in 1933, contracts were let for 500,000 pairs of shoes, 2,500,000 yards of denim, 700,000 pairs of trousers, one million Towels, 300 cars, and three thousand trucks. Can you imagine how many man-hours it took to comply with these contracts at a time when one person out of four was out of work? From 12 to 15 million people directly benefited from enrollees' allotment checks. More than 700 million dollars were sent to families. The entire cost of the corps was almost 3 Billion Dollars.

Also, the CCC enrollees were used extensively in disaster relief. The Ohio-Mississippi river flood of 1937 was a real test. Enrollees built sandbag dikes up and down the rivers and helped rescue and evacuate thousands of flood victims. After the flood waters receded, cleanup was carried out by the CCC. Many other floods of the 1930's were worked by the CCC. The great New England hurricane of 1938 killed more than 500 people and cause more than 400 million dollars in damages. The CCC helped in the cleanup and repaired more than 14,000 houses and buildings. In the greatest hurricane every to strike the Florida Keys on September 2, 1935, the CCC helped cleanup and search for and receive bodies. The CCC suffered its own disaster when Veterans camp, number five on lower Matecumbe Key, was demolished. More than 200 of the 716 veteran enrollees were killed. Their camp was not built to withstand the tremendous wind of the hurricanes.

In many other disaster, from tornadoes, floods, snowstorms and plane crashes, the CCC helped cleanup, rescue, build, repair and retrieve bodies.

The CCC also searched for a kidnapped child in Florida in 1938. The search ended tragically when the child was found dead.

I was pulling my last hitch with the CCC when the organization closed down. I had been shipped to the CCC camp No. 459 at Sand Hill in Columbus, Georgia. Sand Hill CCC camp was located at Ft. Benning Georgia (An Army Base) in Columbus, Georgia. We were quartered in Army barracks, controlled by the Army. My job while at Sand Hill Camp was running the PX (Post Exchange). As things begin to close down, a man by the name of Mr. Babber came into the PX. He introduced himself and said he was in charge of both the Main Officers Club and the PX annex, for the Student Officers who were in Officers Candidate School at Fort Benning.

The PX Annex was located where the students were quartered. He had an opening in the PX Annex and he needed someone with experience to run it. Would I be interested?

"When would I need to start?" I asked.

"I need you now!" He said.

"You know I can't just walk away from here," I said.

"Oh," he said, "But I can take care of it. This CCC camp is run by the Army and will be closing in a few days. If you work with me, today is Thursday I'll have you cleared from the CCC and your quarters prepared. You can move in Sunday and start to work Monday. All you have to do is say you accept the job."

"Mr. Babber I believe you said," I asked, pausing. "How can you be so sure about me? I don't know anything about you and you sure don't know a thing about me!"

"Oh, you're wrong; I know more about you than you think I do. I've already had you checked out. So what do you say we go to the office and drag up a chair and do some talking?"

So we did just that!

When we reached an agreement, Mr. Babber had me cleared from the CCC on Saturday morning, and I moved into my new quarters on Sunday and went to work on Monday, making more money than I had ever dream of making.

The sign says it all.

Civilian Conservation Corps Advertisement

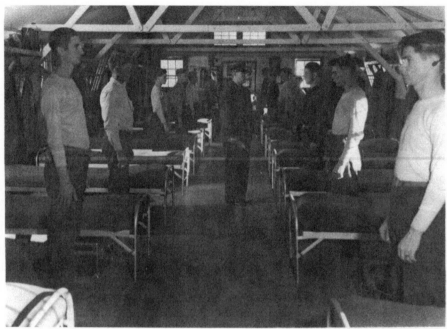

Routine inspections for cleanliness and general appearance and conduct of the young C.C.C. Recruits.

Training to be firefighters.

Building roads in National Forests.

C.C.C. Camp Gilroy, California, Company 450

Retreat at C.C.C Camp, Gilroy, California

Recreation Hall at Camp Gilroy

My discharge papers from the C.C.C's

Monday morning, I got up early, showered and dress. I was excited about my new job and wondering what the other workers were like. I wondered how they'd like someone new coming in and taking over the number one position in the operation of the PX annex, and Club. I pushed these thoughts out of my mind and headed for the Officers Club for breakfast, about a mile from the PX annex. Mr. Babber's driver, Tom, picked me up and took me to and from my meals.

After breakfast, on our way to work, I asked Tom, "How long have you been driving for Mr. Babber?"

"Three years," he said.

"Do you know him very well?"

Tom said, "One of the finest people I've ever worked for. A good Christian and family man. If he tells you something you can count on it. You will find him to be strictly business and he doesn't know what the word humor is. But he's a good man and you will like him."

I said, "He had an opening when he hired me, the number one position in the club. You wouldn't know by chance why the job opened, would you?"

Tom said, "Well here we are. I'm suppose to take you in and introduce you to the others. Mr. Babber said he would be by later today and help you get everything squared away. I must go now, I have another run to make. As far as questions, we'll talk more when I pick you up for lunch."

By this time we were inside the Club door. Two men were very busy serving the morning rush troops. Tom ushered me over to a big guy named Mack. He introduced me. Mack grunted and stuck out his hand. Tom and I met the other man, Julian. Julian stopped and dried his hands.

With a big smile, he shook my hand, "I'm sure glad to see you. We need you."

Tom said, "I'll see you at lunch time which will be 11:30, have to pickup Mr. Babber at 12:30 for lunch. Bye now."

Julian called me over to him. "There's an apron on the shelf you'll need one. Might as well help us out. If you need or can't find anything I'll be glad to help you out."

I put on an apron and went to work. It was around seven o'clock in the morning when the Club opened and closed around nine o'clock p.m. Now the Club annex was located in one of the barracks, in the Officers Candidate School section of the base. There was always a crowd of students before class started. At lunch break it was the same. After retreat, in the evening until closing time, was the busiest time of all. No one could use the Club except students. They could not go to town. The only place they could go was to the club and they came in droves.

At 11:30 a.m. Tom picked me up for lunch.

"Tom," I asked, What about the relief man who comes on at the two p.m. shift? You know; Mr. Smith?"

Tom said, "He's an older married man with a family, living in downtown Columbus. He's been with Mr. B. several years. The other one, Mr. Walker, is a younger man. I don't know how to tell you about him. I just don't know. But I will say this. I would be very, very, careful, in dealing with Mr. Walker. You asked me this morning, by chance would I know why the position became open. Yes I know, but I don't have proof. Bill was a good man. Maybe that was his trouble; he was too good."

I asked, "What do you mean too good?"

"In the club office there's a Safe, we call this the ring safe. This is your office now."

"Why a ring safe?" I asked.

"When an OCS student starts School, there is a ring company that will take the student's order and measurement for the OCS class ring. They make the ring in advance so the student's will have them as soon as school is out. And too, the student can pay on his ring while in school if he wishes to. The ring cannot be issued until graduation, and even then the ring must be paid in full before the issue is made. Of course if a student failed to graduate his money was returned to him if he had paid out any."

"Well this answers my question about the safe." I said.

"Mr. JD, I don't know and don't have any proof—neither does anyone else—but I do know this. I was taking Bill to lunch one day and Bill looked terrible. I asked Bill if problems were piling up on him."

At first he didn't want to talk about it. Then, sometime later, while we were eating, I said again, that he looked troubled, and was there anything I can do?

Then, Bill laid down his fork and stopped eating. He leaned forward on the table and said, "I'm in trouble big time."

I asked, "What about?"

"I don't want to burden you with my problems," Bill said.

I kept on, "Bill, I don't want to push you, but I hate to see you troubled so."

Then Bill began to talk. "Tom, I'm going to tell you something and I don't want you to say anything about it to no one."

Tom said, "If that's what you want, that's what you will get."

Bill said, "About three weeks ago, Walker came to me with a sad story. He needed to put up $500.00 at the hospital to get some medical treatment for his wife. He asked if I would let him have the money. He needed it for only one week because he had money coming in then. But he needed the money the next day."

"Well I didn't have the money to let him have."

He put in on me to let him have the money out of the ring safe, and that he would have it back in there within a week. With all kind of promises of assurance. I gave in and let him have the ring money. I did so without any kind of security, just his word. The class is graduating in two days. I have been notified by the ring Company it will have people here to take ring sizing for the new class, and please have the past accounts cleared and ready to be picked up. Walker told me yesterday that he had the money, and would bring it in today. But he called and said he had to have another day off for he had to take his wife to another Dr. and would not be in until then, and for me to go ahead and get everything ready to turn in for he would for sure be here the next morning."

"Bill," Tom said, "I don't know anything about the man maybe you are just worrying for nothing, lets just hope he will show up tomorrow with the money. So you can replace it before you have to turn in the accounts."

"Man, I sure hope so."

"Well, let's just wait and see, try not to worry."

The next day the ring company came to clear up the accounts, you guessed it, Walker didn't show. In fact he didn't come in until the two p.m. work time the next day. Bill had no choice but to take the money out of the clubs fund, five hundred dollars and put it in the right fund to clear it up. Bill went to Mr. Babber and told him about the money and it would be returned as soon as Mr. Walker returned to work.

"What did Mr. B say?"

"Mr. B was not pleased at all with the transaction especially after learning Bill had not required a receipt of any kind, or proof he let Mr. Walker have the money." Mr. B told Bill. When Mr. Walker shows up call me. Do not say anything to him. You and I will find out what happened together when Mr. Walker came to work at 2 p.m.

"What did Bill do when he came in?" I asked

"Bill went into the office and called Mr. B. He came out and went to work as though nothing had happened. In about an hour Mr. B called me at the Annex Club where I stay when I'm not on a run, saying only three words "Pick me up!"

"When we returned to the club, Mr. B asked Bill and Mr. Walker to go with him to the office. They did and closed the door behind them. They had a discussion that lasted several minutes. When the three of them came out of the office the look on Bill's face told me nothing good came out of that meeting."

"You don't know what went on in the office?"

"No I didn't JD, not at that time. But I know what was done, Bill was let go, Mr. Walker is still working." Tom said.

I asked, "Did anybody ever find out what happened at the meeting?"

Tom said. "Oh yes, lots of people knew what happened. What they don't know was the truth. Before Bill left he told me when Mr. B asked Mr. Walker about the money, Mr. Walker said," what money?" Mr. B said, "The 500 dollars, Bill let you have out of the ring money for Dr. and Hospital bills for you wife."

The man said, "Mr. B, my wife is not even sick. I don't know what he is talking about!"

Mr. B said, "Do you mean to tell me you did not get 500.00 dollars from Bill?"

Mr. Walker said, "Mr. B I'll tell you again I never got 500.00 dollars from Bill. In fact I've never borrowed any money whatsoever from him. If I have, I ask him to show any kind of evidence."

I looked at Tom and asked. "What do you think? Do you think Bill or Mr. Walker is telling the truth?"

"Mr. JD it's like I said. We know what happened. What we don't know is whose story is right. But I will say again, be very careful in dealing with Mr.Walker. I've known Bill the entire three years. I've been here, I've never known him to do or say anything to cause me to think he's not telling the truth. But I don't know Mr. Walker."

Tom and I returned from lunch. We went into the office and sat around talking, mostly getting to know more about each other. Shortly after 2:00 o'clock p.m., Mr. Smith and Mr. Walker came to work; Tom and I went out to meet them. I was introduced to them by Tom. Mr. Smith was a very well mannered gentleman. Mr. Walker, well, maybe I was looking for something I didn't seem to capture.

"Tom got a call to pick up Mr. B. he was coming to the Club so we could have a talk.

While Tom went to get Mr. B., I spent the time talking to Mr. Smith and Mr. Walker, trying to learn something about them. Shortly, Tom returned with Mr. B. When they came into the Club, Mr. B wore a big smile. Following him was Tom, Julian, and Mack. Just as they got to us a lady came in the door. Mr. B said, "This is Miss Ann. She's from the main office. She will watch the store while we have our meeting. So if you all will follow me we will get started."

We went into the office and closed the door. Mr. B sat down at the desk and looked at us. Finally, he said, "Just so there is no misunderstanding as to what I will tolerate in the operation of this Club. We will start on the right foot and then we'll know where we are going. First, I want it clearly understood that Mr. JD is replacing Bill in every respect. And after I tell you what I know about him and why I'm doing this, if you have any objections, let it be known. Or like the old saying, forever hold your piece."

As Mr. B began to tell them, I wondered how he knew so much about me. Then I recalled about a month past, before the CCC closed down, our supply officer for the CCC camp came into the PX where I was working. He was with another man, and they asked me for two cokes. After I served the cokes they sat down at one of the tables. The supply officer had a folder in his hands. He opened it and the two of them and discussed the contents of the folder. This discussion lasted about half an hour, and then they left the PX.

Then I remembered where I had seen Mr. B. I began to think he knew more about me than I did. He made no mention of Bill anymore. I figured if he wanted me to know about Bill he would have told me. Soon, the meeting was over and Mr. B asked, "any questions? " No one said anything.

"If not you may go."

He said to me, "Mr. JD would you mind staying a little longer, I want to talk with you."

"I'll be glad to." I said.

"I just wanted to tell you if you run into anything you can't handle yourself I want to know about it. Far as I know you have a pretty good crew to work with and if you need me I'm only as far away as your telephone."

I said, "Okay." Then we parted our ways.

I stayed on as manager of the PX Annex and Club until I Joined the Army in 1943.

CAPTURED...POW

For many years I had been approached by several organizations and family members asking me to write my story about being a Prisoner of War, (POW) and how it has affected my life, and the lives' of those dear to me.

I thought little about doing so. I felt there was no way anyone can ever begin to understand how it feels to be stripped of every human right and forced to live like an animal.

Over the years, memories of those days and nights of battles, along with becoming a Prisoner of War (POW) haunted me. I didn't feel comfortable sharing my experience to people, for fear I would be thought of as a seeker of pity or for publicity.

Now I'm old. If there's something I can say to help keep my memories in the minds of our young people, then I want to do this.

The price, which was paid for freedom, oh how precious liberty is! So, I feel it's my duty to tell my story. Having been there and given everything I had short of life, I feel it an honor to leave these facts.

The dedication of the WWII Memorial in Washington DC. President Bush was the keynote speaker. Two Presidents who preceded him, Bill Clinton and George H. W. Bush sat side by side on the stage.

In his remarks, President George W. Bush said, "At this place, at this memorial, we acknowledge a debt of longstanding to an entire generation. Americans, those who died, those who fought and worked and grieved and went on. They saved our country and thereby saved the liberty of mankind. And now, I ask every man and woman who saw and lived WWII, every member of the generation to please rise as you are able, and receive the thanks of our great Nation.

America acknowledges a debt beyond our power to repay."

About half of the 17,000 stood up. Many were in wheelchairs, all frail and proud to be recognized for who they are. Tom Brokaw named them the Greatest Generation.

Senator Bob Dole was there. He had been severely wounded in Italy in WWII. He said, "What we dedicate today is not a memorial to war. Rather it is a tribute to the physical and moral courage that makes heroes out of city and farm boys. And that inspires Americans in every generation to lay down their lives for people they will never meet. For ideals that makes life itself worth living."

It is a good feeling when we hear the leaders of our great country; recognize the men and women of our Armed Forces who saved the freedom and liberty of our country.

On certain days of the year, we are reminded of our Patriotism by the display of flags, parades and such. But did you ever stop and wonder just how the price was paid by the sacrifices and blood given by our troops? Oh, I'm sure you have, but I thought maybe you would like to walk along side of me and let you and I get down to where the rubber meets the road. Let's see just what and how the price was paid for this freedom.

I enlisted in the Army in 1943 at Fort McPherson, Georgia. I took basic training at Camp Walters in Texas. After basic training, I was sent to Fort Benning, Georgia for para troop training. Me and jumping out of a plane was not on the same wave length, so I wound up running the horse stable in Ft. Benning, Georgia.

One evening about sunset I was exercising the meanest horse in the stable. I was about a half mile from the stable when the horse got spooked and ran. When I tried to stop him the bit broke the bridle came off of his head and landed in my lap. All I could do was hold on. The horse ran a short distance on the side of the road. Then he decided he'd rather be on the road. And the speed he was going, I knew when he got to the stable, turning off of the newly graveled road, he would fall, and he did.

From that incident, I spent almost a month in the hospital and the horse was injured in the side. When released from the hospital, I was transferred to Fort Jackson, South Carolina to join the newly organized 106th Infantry Division.

I was in Company B, the 423 rd Regiment of the 106th Infantry Division. The division completed training at Fort Jackson and went to North Carolina maneuvers. On completion of maneuvers, the division went by convoy to Camp Atta bury, Indiana to complete our training.

In November 1944, we were shipped overseas. The 106th Infantry Division landed at Le-Havre France at night,

The next morning we loaded into opened trucks, in the cold drizzling rain, and moved out. Some of the men laughed and made jokes about sunny France. Others cursed the rain, sleet, cold and fate, which had brought us to this battle scorned Europe. There were those that said nothing.

In a clump of trees off to one side of the road, stood what once had been a country chateau. It was decayed and rotten now. The bomb cratered ground and shell of the fire gutted house gave evidence of what had passed.

In a field across the road. lay the broken remains of an allied bomber—a military warplane—dead and there was a feeling someone ought to bury it. The scene was dreary and foreboding. The trucks roared over pitted rough roads towards St. Vith, we drove through small towns and battered remnants of villages, past burned skeletons of tanks and trucks in the ditches.

On either side of the road were jeeps, weapon carriers with men sitting in them. Some had their hands on the steering wheel. I wondered why they were just sitting there. As we got closer I saw they had been shot and were frozen in that position. As we moved on, people came out of their houses, smiles, waved and made the "V" for victory sign with their fingers. We would smile and wave back.

As the long convoy winded through the mountains of eastern Belgium and Luxemburg, we saw snow-covered evergreens and thought about Christmas, only a short time off. Then we remembered where we were and why we had come. When we got to Limesy, France the truck ride was over. From Limesy we had a three-day march in the cold rain and snow. Arriving at St. Vith at night we went to our battle position the next day. We relieved the veteran 2nd Inf. Division.

We used the trenches and foxholes of the 2nd Division. I was assigned to a section to cover and a foxhole. In order for me to get into my foxhole, out of the trench, I had to crawl over a bank of dirt. As I did so, I was fired upon. I was hit in the left foot and I rolled back into the trench. As I did, I saw where the shots came from and returned fire. I stopped that one from firing anymore.

Of course with all of the firing going on the trench filled very quickly with troops. When the Medic removed my boot, we found the bullet had gone through the top of the toe of my boot and only grazed the top of my toes. The bullet did not even break the skin. My Commanding Officer congratulated me on being a better shot than the enemy was. He pulled me off the line for the rest of the day.

He said, "After you shoot a man, you need to regroup if you have time to do so."

A patrol was sent out to check for more snipers. In returning to the Command post, (CP), they reported they had found the one who had fired on me, in the direction I had told them.

This was along the Belgium-German frontier. It was somewhat of a quiet section. There had been only light patrol activity and the section was assigned to our Division, the 106th, so it could gain experience.

The baptism of fire to come was the first action for our Division.

And for many it was the last.

The 106th was assigned to the VIII Corps. And took position in a slight arch along the forest covered ridge of the Schnee – Eiffel. (Siegfried Line). Approximately twelve miles west of St. Vith, France with a 27 mile front to defend. The three regiments, (422nd 423rd and 424th) of the 106th division were placed into position. The 14th Calvary Group flanked the North side of the 106th division and the 28th Infantry Division flanked the south side.

I will now quote from Major General Donald A. Stroh, the Commanding Officer's report and my eye witness personal knowledge.

The following events occurred, as reported in the General's report.

General Stroh's report:

When the history of the Ardennes fighting has been written, it will be recorded as one of the great strategic Allied successes of the war in Europe. Tactically, for the 106th and the other American Divisions involved, it was a bitter and costly fight.

But it became increasingly clear the Germans expended in the last futile effort those last reserves of men and material they so badly needed a few months later. The losses and sacrifices of the 106th Division paid great dividends in eventual victory. These pages are dedicated to those gallant men who refused to quit in the darkest hour of the Allied invasion and whose fortitude and heroism turned the tide toward overwhelming victory."

December 16th, 1944

Springing from the bleak vastness of the Schnee-Eifel with the speed of a coiled snake. Field Marshall Von Rundstedt's desperate but mighty counter offensive struck toward Belgium and the Ardennes. Carefully hoarded Panther and Tiger German tanks followed by battle-tested infantry launched the last gamble aimed at shattering the taut lines of the U.S, First Army. Seizing the cities of Liege and Antwerp, and slashing through the Allied forces to the sea.

The full force of this massive attack was thrown against the new, untrained, 106th Infantry Division. But despite the vulnerable 27 mile front and despite inadequate reserve supplies and lack of air support, the valiant men of the Lion Division, so called because our unit emblem was a lions head, the 106th took a tremendous toll of enemy troops. We wrote a story in blood and courage to rank with the Alamo, Chateau-Thierry, Pearl Harbor and Bataan!

They never quit, said Field Marshall Sir Bernard Montgomery said of us, "The American soldiers of the 106th Infantry Division stuck it out and put up a fine performance. By Jove, they stuck it out, those chaps. At St. Vith, first objective of the German thrust, the 106th held on grimly at a time when every hour of resistance was vital to the Allied cause. The 106th fought against superior forces, with pulverizing artillery battering from all sides. It was men against tanks, guts against steel. Their heroism gained precious time for other units to regroup and strike back. In one of the bloodiest battles of the war, the 106th showed the Germans and the world how the American soldiers can fight and die."

During the night of Dec. 15th front line units of the 106th, we noticed activity in the German positions. My company, Co. B, the 423rd Infantry Division, had been on the move since around midnight, December 13, 1944. We reached our destination and were placed on the front line again on December 15th. We were instructed to dig in, although we had no time to dig foxholes. It was around 2:00 a.m. At that time, it was suggested we dig slit trenches, (a slit trench being a ditch long enough to lie down in and deep enough your body will be below the surface of the ground). This protects a soldier from mortar and artillery shells at ground burst.

We started with the small trenching tool, moved the snow and began to dig. We hoped we could beat the odds of having our trenches ready by daybreak.

I had my trench ready around 4:00 or 4:30 a.m. just before daybreak. After being on the go for three days and nights, I had no problem falling asleep in my new bed.

My nap lasted about an hour.

We were rousted out to get a sandwich and coffee, which was the first food and coffee in almost two days and nights. This was the morning of December 16, 1944. At 5:40 a.m. the enemy began laying down a thunderous artillery barrage. We were lined up to receive our sandwich and coffee when all hell broke loose. We dove for cover in our trenches.

Before I could get to my trench, a troop had beaten me to it, so we both dove for the trench, he went in first. I landed on top of him, and someone landed on top of me. After the artillery barrage and mortar shells let up, we began to come out.

The guy on top of me was up and gone. He had been hit but I don't know how bad it was. His bandolier belt of ammunition had been cut from his back and was lying on my back. There was blood on the belt, so I knew he had been hit. Being somewhat offended with the guy under me for taking my trench, I grabbed him rolling him over only to discover over half of his face had been blown away. I thanked God that he had gotten to my trench first.

What had happened was this: at first, fire was directed mainly against the northern flank sector of the 14th Calvary Group, which flanked the north side of the division. Slowly the barrage crept southward, smashing strong points along the whole division front. Treetops snapped like toothpicks under murderous shell burst. "We the 106th Inf. Troops." Burrowed into our holes and fortifications, waited tensely for the attack. The darkness was filled with bursts from medium and heavy field pieces of railway artillery, which had been shoved secretly into position.

The explosions were deafening and grew into a terrifying hell of noise when Nazi's started using their Nebelwerfers "Screaming Meemies".

A *Nebelwerfers* is a six-barrel projector firing six-inch rockets and sits on a base like a mortar. Full weight of the barrage was brought to bear on the 589th Field Artillery Battalion. supporting the 422nd Regiment. Hundreds of rounds bombarded their position in 35 minutes. At 7.00 a.m. the barrage lifted in the forward areas. Now came the attack. Waves of volksgrenadiers, or German Infantry spearheaded by Panzer Tanks, smashed against the division lines in a separate try for a decisive early breakthrough.

They were stopped.

A second attack was thrown against the division. Again the Dough's held. The Nazis threw in wave after wave of fresh troops, replacing their losses. There was no replacement for the 106th Division, the Lion men.

We began to settle our grim business. We dug deeper and fought with everything we had. German bodies piled up often at the very rim of our foxholes. Still the Nazis came. Bodies got higher. We had to get out of our holes, using bodies as shields, while fighting and killing other Wehrmacht soldiers.

Throughout the day, the attacks mounted in fury. Hundreds of fanatical Germans rushed straight toward the American lines, only to be mowed down or driven back by a hail of steel.

Others came on and met the same fate. The deadly, careful fire of the stubborn Lion men of the 106th Infantry Division exacted a dreadful toll on the enemy.

Finally, under pressure of overwhelming numbers, the 14th Calvary Group was forced to withdraw on the north flank giving the Germans their first wedge in the division front. Enemy tanks and Infantry in increasing numbers then hacked at the slowly widening gap in an effort to surround the 422nd Regiment.

In the meantime, a second panzer tank led assault, supported by German Infantry, hammered relentlessly at the 423rd, (my regiment) and the 424th regiment.

Early next morning, a wedge was driven between the two regiments. German columns swung north to join the one that had broken through the 14th Calvary Group section. At this time the 422nd and the 423rd Regiments were surrounded. The 424th was able to pull back to St. Vith, so naturally the Nazis headed for St. Vith.

There the cooks, clerks, truck drivers and mechanics, shouldered weapons and took to the foxholes. Hopelessly out numbered and facing heavier firepower, they dug in for a last ditch defense. Of the key road center. They were joined on December 17, 1944 by Combat Command B 9th Division, and elements of the 7th Armored Division.

Surrounded, the 422nd and the 423rd Regiments fought on. Ammunition and food ran low. Appeals were radioed to Headquarters for supplies to be flown in. But the soupy fog covering the frozen countryside made air transport impossible. The valiant stand of the two fighting regiments inside German lines was proven to be a serious obstacle to the Nazi plan. It forced Von Rundstedt to throw additional reserves into the drive to eliminate the surrounded Americans. This enabled the remaining units and their reinforcements to prepare for the heroic defense of St. Vith. This delayed their attack schedule and prevented the early stages of the Battle of the Bulge from exploding into a complete enemy victory.

Low on ammunition and food gone, the ranks depleted by three days and nights of ceaseless fighting, the 422nd and the 423rd Regiments battled from their fox holes and the old Siegfried line bunker. We fought the ever growing horde of panzers with bazookas, rifles and machine guns. One of our last radio messages was, "Can you get some ammunition through?"

Then no more was heard from the two encircled regiments except news brought back by small groups and individuals who escaped the trap. Many had been killed. Many were missing and turned up later in German Prison Camps.

I asked you earlier to go with me where the rubber meets the road earlier. Well friend, this is it, you have heard the Commanding General's actual report as to what happened. Now lets you and I look at what and how it happened.

Oh, what fighting and dying! Seeing men lose part of their bodies, as we fought in that circle! No food, no rest and very limited ammunition. Every direction you looked the enemy is there in unbelievable force. We had nothing—to speak of—to fight with. You don't fight tanks with rifles and win.

By now, we were surrounded. The 422nd Regiment and my Regiment the 423rd were like ducks sitting on a pond with hunters all around. In every direction you looked you were looking down the barrel of a weapon, knowing the very next second could be our last one on earth. As we look on our left we see young men crying out for help for his mother, sometimes with one or both legs, feet, arms and hands missing and we wouldn't be able to stop and help them. Moving on stepping over bodies, some enemy. Oh yes, Enemy, (When you have to step over men lying wounded, begging you to finish killing them, crying for their mothers, wives and children, and all you can do or want to do is disarm him and walk away, you must remember he's not just an enemy. He's some mother's son, a wife's husband, and a child's father. And only by the grace of God, you are the one walking away.

Again, he's no enemy; he's a person someone cares for.

When I rolled over the man in my trench, so much of his face was gone, you couldn't tell who he was even if you had known him. As we fought to break out of the trap, you could not tell if you were with the

422nd or 423rd troops. Everybody was scared and fighting with any and everything you could put your hands on.

Have you ever been so scared you could not move or speak? I was.

It was about 3:00 a.m. in the morning. We were shifted in position to reinforce the line. There were about six or maybe eight of us. We were in a little ravine for cover. Tracer bullets looked like lightning bugs in the night as we walked along with the group.

Something hit my leg and moved on down to my foot. I put my hand on my ammunition belt and discovered that the phosphate grenade on my belt had dropped on my foot. The grenade safety handle was still hooked to my belt. Now when the safety handle is pulled, you have four to six seconds before the grenade goes off!

I could not speak on move. Other men were around, but I could not warn them.

Time ran out on the explosion. When I finally could move and speak, I examined the handle. The detonator was still attached to the handle. On a white phosphate grenade, the detonator is screwed into the casing. I figured walking, rolling on the ground someway or other may have caused the handle and detonator to work their way out of the casing. I searched and recovered the casing and reassemble it and it sure came in handy later on. I thanked God for watching over me.

At daylight we had to cross an open field. Prior to crossing the field, German tanks opened fire on our position along with artillery. They shelled us with timed fused shells, set to burst at tree top level. We were on the line fighting. We had no foxholes for cover. The only cover we had was to stand very close to the trees, on the backside of the incoming rounds. Now when shells burst at tree top level fragments fall straight down, so you are a smaller target standing upright than lying flat on the ground. Even then, if the fragments don't get you, chances are a treetop or a limb will. It's a blood bath either way you look at it. Those of us left had to cross the open field after the shelling stopped.

We were assembled at the edge of the field. We had no cover whatsoever as we were open targets, I begin to pray and I was not the only one doing so. While we prayed, a Chaplin came up and asked if he could pray for us before we moved out. He didn't have to ask twice. We got on our knees and the Chaplin placed his hands on our head and prayed for each one of us.

They were sending out eight men at a time. We stood there watching the men go out sometimes; half of them would make it, sometimes less, and waited for our time to go.

It came time for my group to cross and we did. If a bullet came close to me, I knew nothing of it.

As we crossed the open field, passing those who didn't make it, we looked into the faces of dying men. We heard their cries for help, and were unable to stop and lend a helping hand or a word of comfort. All we could do was wipe our tears and thank God, we were still moving.

After we crossed the open field, there was just a few of us was left, and I realized I was with a complete bunch of strangers.

Then we ran into what seem like a whole army of Tiger-Tanks. Swinging to our right flank to avoid the tanks, we met the German infantry head-on. As we fought, we gained their foxholes and stoops made mostly from pine logs. At least this would give us some cover.

From the foxholes bodies of Germans piled up, (like the General said in his report.) We could not see the enemy so we came out of the foxholes using the German bodies for shields. Those alive, we disarmed. We saw a pile of bodies, some begging, some crying. We looked into their faces and heard their pleas. I no longer saw an enemy, but some mother's son. Some wife's husband, some child's father. I saw someone who was loved and missed as I was. And all I could do was wipe tears and listen to the sounds that are as vivid today as 65 years ago.

Our small group became shorter and shorter on ammunition. But we were doing well and regrouped and formed a counterattack to break out of the steel trap. This was called the bold thrust counterattack because we were blocked by the sheer weight of German numbers, tanks and German infantry. Soon we ran out of ammunition. We delayed tanks by laying in ditches after the tank passed over us. We slowed them down sometimes stopping them with firebombs made with bottles of gas and fire. With our rifles we kept the tanks buckled up so their field of fire was very limited. During this time, we had no food, for days and nights. I don't recall how many. We had no rest and no ammunition.

I remember firing my last round of ammunition. I then disassembled my weapon, throwing the parts in all different directions. I held rifle by the barrel and wrapped it around a tree then threw the stock in one directions and the barrel in the other. With no weapon, I took cover in the wooded area. I roamed, trying to get a bearing on where I was and how to get through enemy lines and back to friendly troops. I didn't know where I was or what time it was, for in battle time comes only twice in 24 hours. You know when its day, and you know when it's night. All the rest of the time makes no difference.

I did figure it to be somewhere around mid-afternoon. I found myself trying to sneak by a German machine gun position with two guards. I already had three strikes against me and it was still daylight. I only had a bayonet. The Germans were hunched over a bucket of hot coals eating sausage and bread. I was so hungry and cold, temptation almost got the best of me. But common judgment won out so I turned and went another way.

I got maybe three hundred feet and heard groan's coming from some tall weeds and brush. I identified the man as an American and made myself known. The man was injured and I placed a tourniquet on his leg. Most of his foot was missing and the other leg was broken just below the knee.

I gave him all the assistance I could and he pointed in a direction. He said, "If you can make it through the enemy lines, go in that direction and you will find friendly forces."

I told him I would hang around until someone came to give him the help he needed.

He said, "Soldier, we have nothing to fight with. He pulled his jacket open and exposed a set of Captain's bars. And that's an order."

You guessed it. I went right back in the direction of the German machine gun nest. After days and nights. Trying to break through, I realized everyman was on his own. All I had was a bayonet and my two feet. By now it was almost night. I figured I would have a much better chance of getting by the machine gun now. I hoped I would not have a problem with just one man on the machine gun.

After night fell I made my way by the machine gun position. And it must have been around 2:30 a.m. in the morning. When I ran into friendly troops. My hopes jumped a thousand points but it didn't take long for the air to come out of my balloon. I had rejoined my own outfit.

They had pulled back our line position.

My Company B, (106th Infantry Division) was on the western mountain slope, confronting another higher ridge upon which was located Bransheid, a hamlet- like town with a glistening church steeple. We occupied Siegfried line pillboxes on our hilltop with the enemy doing likewise on their slope. They had pulled back into a perimeter and organized to counter attack through Schonberg with the mission to regroup with the Division at St. Vith.

My B Company, was designated as 1st Battalion point to take and hold the Schonberg Bridge, the two regiments could regroup with the division at St. Vith. While awaiting orders to move out Joe our company messenger, told the group where he was and what he was doing when the battle begin and he got his baptism of fire.

Oddly enough, my baptism of fire came while I was defecating over a slit trench when suddenly the earth about me began to tremble. I was in an exposed position with enemy shells coming in. Well I grabbed my rifle, without pulling up my pants, and made for are platoon pillbox jumping in headfirst. In a way, this served as a pressure relief valve because it provided a laugh at a most critical time.

Another of my noteworthy initial encounters occurred when PFC Gordon Piney and I were bringing a case of grenades forward while crossing a logging road. An enemy sniper literally shot my helmet off! Thankfully with no harm to me other than scared beyond description. It wasn't long until being shot at, existing under shellfire and constant bombing raids became matter of course, but it was always stomach knotting.

Joe and I were in the same company. He was with the 2nd platoon, I was in the 1st, Joe's job was completely different from any other in the company. He had his weapon and was trained to use it. Joe spent most of his time in a jeep on open roads, exposed to enemy fire. He delivered and received messages for the Company Commander. And it stands to reason he was involved and knew more about the administration part of the war on company level then we in the foxholes knew.

I had not known where Joe was when the battle started. We had been fighting three days and nights when his story finally came to light. And he was so right, when he said a few yards of separation in battle could change the complexity of the moment. Those of us who survived that climatic battle, mostly wounded, exhausted and battle weary, had a different version of what happened to Company B. A few yards of separation between squads and platoons in a forest did in fact change the complexity of the moment. We had no idea about troop disposition or deployment other than the location of our foxholes, platoon pillbox and company Command Post. We had been told in two weeks we would rotate back to division reserve in time for Christmas.

You have to remember that a lot of us were nothing more than cadet like soldiers. Others had only completed their basic training weeks before. We had no idea as we waved to Lt. Parker, a former company officer transferred to division headquarters, while crossing the bridge at Schonberg that it was not only the single entry to but also the only exit from the position we occupied. We did know our division replaced the 2nd U.S. Infantry division unit for unit, gun for gun, in the western side of the Siegfried Line on what we later learned was called the Schnee Eiffel. This was an isolated mountainous sector accessible only by one bridge across the River Orr at Schonberg. Our Commanding General had immediately questioned the deployment order because of obvious threat for two regiments to be easily surrounded if attacked. However, high command allowed for no revision or *No yielding of conquered German Homeland territory.*

They said it was important to high command because it was the initial intrusion into German homeland by Allied Forces which had been taken in early fall by the 4th Infantry Division.

Another of my noteworthy initial encounters occurred while escorting our Company Commander from our platoon to the Company Command Post. I was guiding him through about 400 yards of heavy enemy artillery bombardment. As we approached the CP, the perimeter guard challenged us. Upon giving the password, we learned the guard had a grenade ready to throw and had discarded the safety pin. With him and us in a rather nervous panic, the Captain ordered me to lead him to a safe area to release the grenade. This was a difficult task in a heavily wooded area while under intense incoming artillery.

Nevertheless, I led him to a ravine, directed he rolled rather then throw the grenade down the incline as we sought cover behind a dirt embankment. It turned out the grenade was a dud, but nevertheless it was a very nerve racking incident.

I had no idea during those predawn hours of December 16, 1944 that the biggest battle of the war was unfolding. It was our misconception in ranks that the Germans were beaten and our combat time would be short-lived. That we'd become part of the Army occupation.

How wrong we were.

After another barrage of artillery let up, Lt. Garwood and Sergeant Ussery traveled back to the Battalion Supply point to scrounge some extra ammo. After dark Lt. Garwood put together a small patrol, of which I was a part, to bring back a supply of ammo and food to our pillbox. (Restocking had to be done at night because the approach was totally exposed to the enemy on the opposite hill.)

The experience was always scary because flares from both sides completely illuminated the area. We had to remain perfectly still with each burst because any movement or noise would draw enemy fire. As yet, we had no idea the pre-dawn heavy artillery barrage of the previous days were actually an all out Hitler inspired counter attack.

Around mid morning an enemy infantry force attacked our unit. Coming under our firepower, they hastily withdrew. We were told not to worry because the 7th Armored Division was on its way to help us. In reality, the 7th was well over sixty miles away and offered no immediate help to us.

After dark the enemy again pounded us with artillery and mortar bombardment. The Germans infiltrated our sound power lines, confusing our communications with Kraut gibberish.

Combined with the artillery damage to our phone lines, this limited our communications as to what the messengers were able to hand deliver. It was a hectic night and I became completely exhausted. Joe was also past going. Lieutenant Garwood told us to take a bunk in the back of the bunker and get some sleep.

It seems as soon as we fell asleep, Sergeant Ussery started shaking us.

Joe said, "The Lieutenant told us to get some sleep and we were going to."

The Sergeant said, "Well you can sleep, but the rest of us is moving out."

It took a moment for his remark to penetrate. We jump up to see our platoon forming to move out. I quickly grabbed my rifle and combat pack and joined the group, already on the move. Our company joined the main line of the march as battalion reserve and provided rear guard support, per orders. The 2nd squad was left in the Brandscheid bunker to cover the rest of the unit disengaging. Joe was in the 2nd platoon and was positioned at the tail end of the platoon walking two abreast with Sack Owens.

About a mile out the column stopped. At that time, we were unaware the lead company had come under attack. Lt. Garwood came and took me and Joe back about 50 yards to serve as rear guard. In the meantime, he shared a password with us because he was going back to get the squad we had left behind. Soon however the march resumed with T/Sgt. Bill at the helm of our platoon because Lt. Garwood had not returned. Joe and I were ordered back to our position in the company. Our march was sporadically interrupted as small arms fire broke out at the front column on a very narrow country road. Although at times we did have to break out across country, in the meantime, thankfully, Lt. Garwood returned with the squad.

Lt. Garwood had been ordered to take his platoon into a higher wooded area and act as left flank guard for the column, which had stopped for a rest. Darkness moved in fast. Within the hour Captain Moore, our Company Commander ordered Lt. Garwood to return with his platoon because the forward march was to resume within minutes. Garwood joined the march with his platoon.

At one point, we came to a "T" in the road and the column turned left. Along with three others, I set up a roadblock to interrupt any enemy approach. It felt like an eternity, but in a few minutes, word came for us to join the main body.

As the column made it up a very steep hillside, we were disbursed into unit bivouac area. We were ordered to sack out for the night. No fires no cigarette lighting and no noise was permitted other than whispers. By now most of us had discarded gas masks and packs, but wisely had kept our trenching tools and weapons.

All we could do was lie on cold ground and bunch up pine needles to serve as pillows. It was severely cold. Apparently, I fell asleep because I was awakened by men digging foxholes. for themselves. I started digging, but with tree roots and frozen ground, this was an almost impossible task.

A recently arrived private, next to me, had discarded his trenching tool with his pack during the up hill march and was getting a kick out of the rest of us trying to dig into the unyielding ground. But when the continuing barrage of incoming artillery began, he begged us to loan him our tool.

The Germans zeroed in on our digging noise and began an intense artillery barrage. The incoming 88s and tree bursts drenched the area. Between the bursts of fire, we'd share our tools with the newcomer. But the ground was frozen hard. All we could do was ball up in fetal positions and pray. During this German artillery barrage, our Battalion Commander was fatally wounded and our first sergeant went heroic or hysteric!

He began yelling, "I guess I don't have to remind B Company men to put their helmets on now!" A constant complaint during training was that our troops would take off their helmets because of weight and discomfort.

It seems now, this artillery barrage would never stop. But it finally did. And amid horrific cries of pain, pleas to Mom and loud prayers we were ordered to move out. In those days we had been indoctrinated to leave our casualties behind for the follow up medics to take care of.

We reassembled in an open area in the woods and Joe accompanied our Company Commander to a battalion escape plan briefing. Counter attack was planned by S3 Officer Alan Jones. We went into attack formation to break out of the pocket and join the division. But due to the exigencies of the situation our facts became disjointed. On the Schonberg breakout attack I, JD Lankford, was there. With unbelievable German forces of fresh infantryman and tanks. We had no other choice but counter attack.

It was clearly understood that if we were unable to breakout, we would hold the position as long as possible. This would allow the other allied forces to reorganize and stop the enemy attack. Company B 423rd, moved out with the 1st and 2nd platoons leading the way. I was in the 1st platoon, and Joe was in the second.

When Joe and the others set up a roadblock to guard the rear, my platoon advanced and came face to face with the enemy. Therefore, we were the first to draw fire. Not only from infantrymen rifle fire, but tanks, anti aircraft guns, oh Lord, the devastating incoming artillery firepower and tree top bursts, we were exposed on the hillside to direct bombardment and there's just no way to explain the agony, the pain and fright. It was another blood bath.

Just as we came out of the line of trees, we met a German anti craft unit digging into our front. They immediately opened up on us with direct fire. Tanks to our right did like wise. I dropped into a slight gully, along with two maybe three other men, and best I can recall I think the other men was out of the 2nd platoon. At such a time you don't stop and introduce yourself. Every man is fighting for his life; scrambling for cover. Our return of rifle fire was haphazard and useless as pandemonium took over. With the devastating incoming firepower and tree bursts, it was agony again because we were exposed on the hillside with no means of effective return firepower. Almost everyone in our group was hit.

The worst injured was a private from the other platoon whose leg was blown off above his knee, and a fellow named Bradley, whose rump wound up with another opening. When the firing ceased somewhat, Burp-gun armed Germans were all over the roadway.

They yelled at us, eyeball to eyeball, "Come out to the road or be killed."

In apparent shock, we melted away as a fighting unit as one followed another with our hands interlocked behind their necks.

Captain More, our Company Commander, was on my right. A short distance away. One of the Germans recognized him as an officer. He was quickly separated from us and whisked away. To my left around twenty feet, PFC. Gilbert and some of his squad came face to face with a Tiger Tank. They were ordered to halt by the tank Commander.

PFC Forbes a man in Gilbert's squad and standing fifteen or twenty feet away raised his M1 rifle and shot and killed the tank Commander at point blank. During the confusion, the rest of the squad, me included, escaped into the woods.

I quickly became separated from the others, for a time, it was every man on his own. I don't know when, how or what happened to the rest of them.

We were fighting some were dying, as we saw men loose body parts and lives. We fought for delay in time which was so badly needed. We had no, rest, or sleep. No ammunition and everywhere I looked, the enemy was there in unbelievable force and us with nothing to speak of, to fight with. You can't fight Tanks with rifles and win.

Earlier in the story, I asked you to go with me where the rubber meets the road, well friend, this is it. You have heard the Commanding General's report, some of mine and others who were there as to what happened. Now, let's you and I step back just a little and take a closer look at some of the things that happened.

As you know by now, we were surrounded. We were sitting ducks on an open pond, with hunters all around, in all directions we looked down the barrel of weapons, knowing the very next moment could be our last one on earth. As we walk a young man in pain on the left cried out for his mother, father and sometimes his children. Sometimes the fallen had one, sometimes both legs blown off or feet and hands missing. We move on, stepping over bodies, some of them our brothers in arms, others, the enemy.

Now Walk With Me into battle, but don't get involved; you won't like it.

Cpl. Rogers, PFC. Black and I along with one other whose identity I never learned, were assigned to hold a vital road junction against three Tiger Tanks supported by infantry. All we had was a machine gun, rocket launcher, two rifles and a carbine. We volunteered to guard the rear. We stopped the advance forces and held the enemy at bay for two and a half hours. We retreated only when the machine gun failed to function. We moved back and found cover along with most of the platoon in an empty house near Schonberg, that didn't turnout very well.

It wasn't very long before the platoon was pinned down in the house by a couple of tanks and infantry. All was doomed unless we could escape. And that could only happen if the enemy's attention could be diverted. Again it was a volunteer mission! Pfc. Jones picked up a sub machine gun, went outside, faced the enemy with such a commotion, the platoon withdrew safely from the rear of the house. When last seen, Pfc. Jones was pouring fire into the German infantry. He was listed as Missing In Action until April, 1945, when he turned up in a POW camp.

He was awarded the Distinguish Service Cross. As the drive of the crushing force of the Nazis ground into our surrounded units, a lot of men were killed and/or captured.

One of the most magnificent bluffs I ever witnessed was when Captain Lee talked 102 German soldiers, including two Germans officers, into surrendering an almost impregnable position to a hand full of American soldiers. Capt. Lee walked boldly to the very muzzle of enemy machine gun to warn them of the Huge Force Supporting him and ordered the senior officer to surrender.

To everyone's surprise, it worked!

When we were trapped, many men and small groups made desperate attempts to cut their way out and a few made it. Among the few I was attached to who attempted to cut out, only three I know of made it. I don't know the number killed or captured. And I don't know the number that was in the group with us, but I do know Capt. Murray, Sergeant Walter and myself were there.

All I can say is we sure had a night.

We made the cut or thought we had for a while. We started for the American lines.

There was a bridge over the Our River and we had to walk across or swim. In the middle of December we thought it a little to cold to go swimming, so our choice was the bridge.

When we got to the bridge we had company. Three Germans were guarding the bridge, so it was fight or by-pass the bridge. The guards were sitting around a heated bucket of coals. We could by-pass, by going through an enemy motor pool and Radar Station. We by-passed the bridge and made it through the motor pool. Outside the Radar station we spotted three guards and there seemed no way to get by them.

The Captain said, "If we are going to get by we are going to have to take them out in silence.

"There are three of them, and three of us," said Sergeant Walter.

"Someone said, "no problem."

But it was a problem to me. We paired off and cleared the way, moving on, thinking maybe we might make it through the enemy line. We had not moved over 100 yards when two Germans rose from a foxhole blocking our way. Sgt. Walter solved that problem with his rifle and all hell broke loose.

We faced tanks, artillery crews, and a heavily armed combat patrol sent out to track us down. It being night and the forest thick with underbrush, the combat patrol was hard to shake. We played cat and mouse with them for a long time. Sometimes we were so close to the enemy we could almost hear them breathing. They were so close at times we could have touched them. Finally we were able to shake the patrol. We realized then we would never make it through and the only chance we had was to try and make it back where we started from our troops in the circle.

After almost three hours crawling among enemy lines, we wound up by the bridge where the guards were. To take them out in silence was out of the question for we could not get to them with out being noticed. To fire upon them would have alerted the combat patrol and we'd had enough of them for one night. We figured going back through the motor pool would be our best chance of making it. We knew the patrol and Lord knows who, or what else was looking for us. SO, back through the motor pool we went. Without any trouble we made it back, but we jumped out of the frying pan into the fire.

I found a quiet hole and grabbed a few hours of sleep only to be rousted by artillery fire. An artillery shell hit the base of the mortar we had, rendering it unserviceable. Pfc. Arvannis took the mortar tube, holding it between his legs and aimed by hand. He fired some 15 or 20 rounds when he noticed a squad of German infantrymen creeping towards our position. Training the mortar on them, he shot the last round of ammunition he had and disabled eight of the attackers. The other four rose to their feet and lunged at him in a bayonet charge. He and his assistant gunner emptied their service pistol, stopping three of them. The fourth was on him, bayonet gleaming. The only thing Arvannis had left to fight with was an empty pistol. He faced the bayonet charge and used his pistol as a hammer, beat the German to death.

Other units which in the face of over whelming odds were the 106th QM. Co. 106th Signal Co. 106th Division Band. And 106th 331 Medical Battalion. Later each unit received the Meritorious Service Unit Plaque.

Despite intense enemy artillery and small arms fire, the MP platoon kept the traffic flowing and performed other duties during the counter offensive When the shelling by the was at it's heaviest, the men at traffic post were forced to take a prone position. But these men stuck to their post and directed traffic during this critical period. Over 600 POW's were handled by the MP platoon after St. Vith fell to the enemy. All remaining POW's were marched to Vielsam under cover of darkness and this was accomplished without the loss of a single prisoner.

Members of the MP platoon were called on to conduct ammunition supplies over routes under constant fire. They helped stragglers get back to their units and into the fight. The MP's reconnoitered road, manned roadblocks; crippled tank sand destroyed enemy staff cars with its officers.

My friend, everybody was involved in the fight, trying to break out and holding the enemy at bay while allowing our troops to regroup. If you could fire a weapon, you fired a weapon as long as you had ammunition. Then you fought with empty guns, sticks.

Ration shortage was critical due to enemy advance and destruction of supply depots. Trucks were to find a depot still open. One was located at Dinant, Belgium. The trucks were sent in series. The first six made the trip without any problem, the other six ran into a furious tank battle near St. Hubert, Belgium. They detoured to avoid destruction and got through a day later.

Later they returned with some supplies (not very many), but

anything was better than nothing. As the fury of the battle mounted, maintenance of communication became literally a matter of life and death. The skill and courage of the signalmen of the 106th Signal Co. kept the vital communication lines open whenever humanly possible. Again and again, through the whole division sector, troubleshooters made emergency repairs on lines severed by artillery fire. For signalmen, field splices under enemy fire became commonplace. At times, new lines had to be run through territory teeming with enemy patrols. We were trying to fight our way out, while the town Schonberg, France was under heavy bombardment by the German tanks and artillery.

The trucks from the depot had some gas so we made firebombs to fight tanks with. The bombs sure came in handy.

Now I had been in the forest about three hours trying to get out. But again was unable to do so and I wound up with (only the Lord knew who they were) and their unit. All I knew was they were Americans. They were trying like I was, to survive. Then two tanks near Schonberg, pinned down the unit.

About that time, a Cpl. I had never seen before looked at me said. "Have you ever helped knock out a tank before?"

"No," I said.

"Now is the time to learn. Follow us," he said one more man was with him.

The Cpl. said, "First. we have to get to the back of the tank. You two keep the tank closed up with your rifle fire. I'll mount the tank with the bomb. Someway I'll get the firebomb into the tank. When I do, they'll come out of there. Only two ways to get out of the tank one is the top hatch. The other escape hatch is in the bottom of the tank." Looking at me, he said "You cover the bottom and you," looking at the other man. "Cover the top hatch. After I fire things up I'll hit the ground taking cover on the side of the tank, you two cover me. Don't let anyone out of the tank."

The Cpl. looked very stern at the two of us. He said, "This is not going to be easy but both of you know what must be done. We have no choice but take out those tanks or at least one of them. And not just for us. The entire unit is pinned down and depending on us, if any of us are to survive. If we cannot get to the tank from the rear we have to get into one of the trenches and wait until the tank passes over us. Then attack from the rear."

We saw we could not get to the rear to make the attack. So we worked our way into a trench that was in the path of one of the tanks. We didn't wait long before we had somewhere between 75 to 90 tons of steel passed over us. As soon as the tank cleared the trench, the Cpl. Jumped out of the trench and mounted the tank from the rear.

The other man and I remained in the trench for cover. The next thing I knew, the tank was on fire. Only two men were trying to get out. One came out the top and was stopped. The other crawled from under the tank. He was stopped. In the meantime the Cpl. hit the ground and took cover as planned.

After we saw no more action around the tank, the Cpl. came back to the trench where the other guy and I were. He smiled and said. "Wasn't to bad was it?" (He got no answer).

In another incident, four men of the signal unit stayed at their switchboard while the building was blown up around them. A shell ripped off the rear of the structure and another reduced the right side to rubble. The roof collapsed as the third shell tore into the structure. Still the men stayed at their posts. A fourth shell fell behind the switchboard and wounded two of the operators. They destroyed the board and the signal men withdrew only when ordered to leave by a Superior Officer.

Also, the Medics of the 106th Division distinguished themselves in the bloody battle in the Ardennes forest. One of them was T/5 Walker from N.C. He made several trips by jeep into German territory to recue wounded American soldiers and returned them to the Aid Station. Another Capt. Antrim discovered that deep snow, rough terrain and roving enemy patrols prevented litter bearers from bringing wounded to his Aid Station fast enough. So Captain Antrim packed equipment on his back and went forward to treat them where they fell.

The 331st Medical Battalion also followed the *Survive above Self motto*. Then supported the 422nd, 423rd and the 424th Regiments, respectively, treating and evacuating the wounded.

Two other units of the division were praised for a difficult job well done. The 806th ordinance Co. and the 106th Division Band. Which worked under trying conditions. These men fought like infantrymen in defense of St. Vith.

December 19th-21st 1944, the 112 Combat Team of the 28th Division, was on the right flank of the 106th Division and was cut off from its own division. The 112 Combat Team was attached to the 106th with the 424th Regiment. The 112 Combat Team and the 424th

Regiment held against German attacks south of St. Vith. LT. Col. Thomas J. Riggs was Commander of the 81st Engineer Combat Battalion.

The day after the Battle of the Bulge on, December 16, 1944 and the 17th, Col. Riggs took over the defense of St. Vith with the men he had left of his own battalion, the defense platoon. The 106th Headquarters' Company and the elements of the 168th Engineers waited for the coming blow. The wait was short.

A battalion of German infantry arrived and attacked behind Tiger Tanks. The Germans soon learned they could not break through the 81st Engineer's line of defense. More tanks and infantry were used by the Germans probed for a weak spot in the line. During these attacks, Col. Riggs was in the center of the defense, rallying his men, and personally heading the counter–thrust to keep the enemy off balance. Col. Riggs was captured while leading a patrol in the defense of St. Vith. He was marched across Germany and escaped near the Polish Border. He made his way to the frontier and was sheltered by civilians. He then joined an advancing Red Army (Russian Army) Tank outfit.

After fighting with it several days, he was evacuated to Odessa and from there to Marseilles. Col. Riggs rejoined the 81st, Engineer's in the spring when it was stationed near Rennes France.

I was never with my company any more after my platoon led out from Schonberg and Pfc. Forbs killed that tank Commander and we escaped into the forest. That was the last time I saw anyone from my company until I got captured.

I tried again and again to break out of the trap. It must have been around 10:00 p.m. when I left. I did very well the rest of the night and most of the day outfoxing the enemy. It was almost dark and I was feeling pretty good about myself. I had hope. I was moving down a ravine under the cover of heavy brush when I heard someone call my name. I could not remember when I'd heard my name called last so I turned and approached him.

It was our company clerk. His left foot was almost gone. All that was left was a small piece of his foot sticking to the bottom of his boot. He had bled so much he was as pale as cotton. I removed his belt and applied it to his leg and stopped the bleeding. Some movement appeared over my shoulder. As I turned to see, I met the butt of a German rifle in my right eye. I was loaded into a small truck; I passed out and remained unconscious until I came to in a German Aid station.

Everything I had was gone. Even my boots socks and over coat. The German doctor bandaged my eye and asked me if I knew where I was. I answered no. He informed me I was a prisoner of war and had been dropped off at his station by two German soldiers.

I ask," Where are my boots, socks and coat?"

He said, "This is how you came into my station."

The German doctor spoke very good English. He asked me when was the last time I had anything to eat. I told him I could not remember the last time I had eaten. He gave me a hard tack (German cracker or cookie) and something he called coffee. It was hot and I was glad to get it. At this time, some of our men were being captured and the doctor told me he would have to send me along with the next bunch of prisoners.

I asked him if he could help me with some boots and socks or something. I could not go out in the snow without something on my feet. The doctor could not find any shoes, boots or socks. The only thing he found was an old pair of rubber galoshes. They were too large for me but we tore strips from an old blanket and wrapped my feet with them. I slipped the galoshes on and waited for the next prisoners to come by.

I still don't know what happed to the man I was helping when I was taken out. He wasn't at the German Aid station while I was there.

It was around mid morning when I was turn over to the guards moving prisoners. We walked the rest of the day and were huddled in a field for the night. We slept in piles on each other to keep from freezing to death. We had no blankets, only the clothes on our backs. Those of us with no overcoats would share with one who had a coat by opening the coat and laying it on the ground. The two of us would lie on the coat. Others would lie around and on top of us to keep us warm.

At daybreak. we started walking again. Several days later, we reached a railroad station where we were put into groups of eighty men into boxcars. The cars were very small and had been used to haul horses. They had not been cleaned out. There was not enough room for the men to sit down so half sat and half stood. We rotated sitting and standing, which did not work to well. Finally, we paired off one on one so we could rotate at will.

The boxcars had one small window in the upper back corner. We could see out by standing on our toes, but even then, vision was very limited. We were forced to use one corner of the car for a toilet. There was no cleaning material or anyway to dispose of the waste. We lived like animals in a cage with every human right stripped away. You can't imagine the stench after days and nights, sometimes over a week at the time, in those boxcars.

Food was something of the past. And the only water we had was from eating snow which you only got when transferring from one train to another.

On Christmas night, December 25, 1944, the train pulled into a station. We were in hopes of something to eat and water to drink. But wrong again. No food. No water. We had been there maybe half an hour when the train began moving our cars around. I understood there were twenty-one cars in the train, where we were, I had no idea. But this I do know, after dark on Christmas night, our train moved the boxcars around back and forth and switched the train's directions on several occasions for what seemed like a couple of hours. Then everything stopped.

There was not a sound to be heard except the engine being disconnected from the boxcars and pulling away. We could see small lights on the side of the tracks. We learned later, the lights were on both sides of the boxcars.

It wasn't long before we learned why those lights had been placed there. As we stood and sat in silence, no one making a sound, we wondered why the lights were on when everything should be blackout. Oh yes, we wondered how to prepare ourselves for whatever might take place.

Well it wasn't long before we learned why the lights were on. And why we had been left alone in those boxcars with no engine to move us.

The first break in silence was roar of airplanes.

Next we heard the screaming of bombs coming down. Then bombs hit and exploded all around the boxcars. I, and I'm sure everyone in the boxcars, realized we had been sacrificed.

There was nothing we could do but wait and pray the bombs would miss their mark. Two did not miss. One hit a boxcar only two boxcars from my car. The other hit a car at the end of the line. When the bombs exploded, the pressure from the bombs almost blew the cars off of the tracks. The car I was in had holes torn in the walls large enough you could put a gallon bucket through them. Casualties were everywhere.

The man sitting next to me had a hole in his stomach you could put your fist in. All I could do was sit there, and hold my relief partner in my arms with bombs falling all around. There was no doubt in my mind the next explosive would get me. Some of the men cried, screamed, prayed and called for their mothers and families. I sat there listening to the bombs screaming on the way down, knowing what was going to happen and my whole life flashed before my eyes.

Of course, the most extreme conditions create extreme emotions. Memory of these emotions is inescapable. The things I saw and experienced that night still lives with me sixty-five years later: Locked in cages like animals, expecting death any second, men crying calling for their mothers. Some was going completely out of their mind.

I was forced to hold my rotation partner down, and he still lost it.

After the boxcars were bombed many had been wounded. We'd had another blood bath with no means to clean up and no medical care. We spent Christmas night holding each other, grunting, moaning, crying, praying and thanking God we had survived only to face another round.

It was after Christmas day and way into the next night before we were out of the cars. We walked across the tracks and were forced into another boxcar, leaving the dead and seriously wounded behind.

As we moved from one boxcar to another we grabbed snow, (with train soot, trash and all) and ate it. It had been days since we'd had food or water. In fact, the last time I had anything to eat, it was the hardtack cracker the doctor had given me back at the aid station right after I was captured. My feet were blistered and bleeding from walking with those strips of blanket wrapped around my feet in those too-big rubber galoshes.

We remained where we had been bombed the rest of the night. Around noon the next day we were moved again. I can't recall how many days and nights we were on the train locked up like animals. Under those conditions we became numb and didn't function right. Everything slowed down, especially our thinking.

I do know, somewhere along the line, we were side tracked again and became afraid we would face the same thing we had on Christmas Eve night.

We were lucky. This time we were stranded about three hours before they hooked another engine to the cars. We were on our way again.

Sometime in the morning of late January 1945, we finally reached our destination at Bad Orb (a small town) Germany. We were in such a weak, horrible, debilitated condition, we had an awful time making it up the hill to camp.

When we came out of the boxcar we were like a bunch of hogs going for a feed trough. We buried ourselves in the snow for water, as we'd had no water for over a week while in the boxcars.

The guards were older men from the home guard and they were not in any hurry to stop us from eating snow. Finally they fired shots into the air to get our attention. We were rounded up and headed up the mountain approximately four miles. The old guards were actually good helping us get to camp. They moved us a short distance at a time, stopped, let those who had fallen and couldn't make it any further get up. They allowed us to give them a helping hand. Almost half the soldiers had to have help making it to camp.

The old guards did not mistreat a single prisoner, as far as I know. With them trying to help us the best they could, we almost felt like human beings. But when we got to the P.O.W. camp. it was a different story.

Our guards had told us that soon as we were registered in a POW camp we would receive food, medical help and clothing. We would be in a camp, no more walking, no more bombs or being locked in a boxcar. Warm food and clothing at last; the war would be over for us.

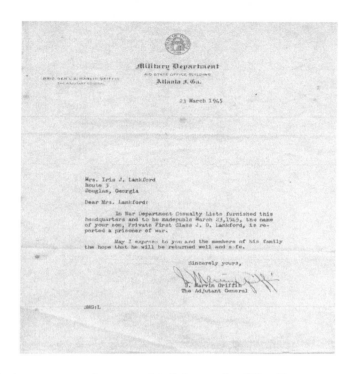

**Letter my mother received from the War Department
that I was a Prisoner of War**

J.D. Lankford

Telegram to my mother informing her I was a Prisoner of War

Prisoner of War camp Headquarters, Stalag IXB in Bad Orb, Germany

The building to your far right is #42; this is where I spent my time as a POW

Stalag 9B P.O.W. Barracks

J.D. Lankford

P.O.W.'s celebrate their liberation.

Mildred, J.D. Ronnie and Donnie our boys and our tour guide.

This is the building where we stood with machines guns pointed at us from midnight until the break of day. Expecting to be mowed down at any moment.

Pool where we were forced to drink water when the water system wasn't working. The building was where we were interrogated.

Lankford's 51 Chevrolet in front of building #42 where I stayed while a P.O.W.

**J.D. AND Mildred Lankford at the building
where I was held captive**

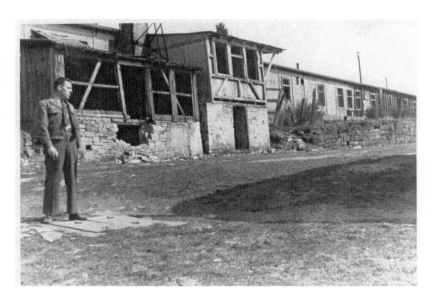

J.D. Lankford in front of the kitchen

This stove was used for soup while we had it. The rest of the time to warm water for what they called coffee.

These are concrete boilers used to serve what soup we got

This is where we received our soup until it runs out, bread, one loaf until it was out and then one small potato.

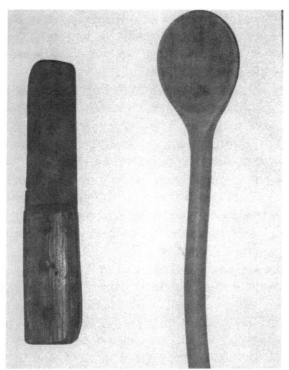

Knife and Wood Spoon I made in P.O.W. Camp, I never got to use the spoon, they ran out of soup.

We got another big surprise.

When we got into camp it was a different story. I don't know if it was true or not, but I was told the prison camp commander was an ex-SS Trooper, (Schutzstaffel, German for protection Squadron). Some of the things he initiated sure fit the claim. I was put in building No. 42, one of three large masonry barracks. It had its advantage; one being that one end of the building had been placed in a slot dug out of the mountain. The building was protected from the wind and sleet and protected from air fights. (When American planes got into dogfights with German planes the Germans flew over the POW camp so our allied planes would stop chasing and firing at them).

We placed large rocks on the ground spelling out P.O.W. On several occasions, the planes would be well over the camp before they saw the sign. Around noon one day, several weeks after we had been in camp two men were killed inside one of the buildings and the clock on the tower got shot up.

In the No.42 building there was no running water, no bath facilities and no inside toilet. We used a trench on the outside of the building with logs across it to sit on. There was also no wood for the small heater in the middle for the building.

Beds lined each side of the building with an aisle down the middle. The beds were bunk beds stacked four high made from poles for the bed post. The bottom of the beds was made by four six inch pine boards. We were given a mattress stuffed with some kind of straw which just fit the bed. No pillow and one blanket.

My bed was the second from the bottom. That first day we got our beds, blankets and mattress it was almost night. We were roused out of the building and marched down to the kitchen to get some food. It was half a canteen cup of potatoes and cabbage soup. The potatoes were rotten and the cabbage looked and tasted like garbage, but it was hot. I'd had no idea how long it had been since I had anything to eat. At the kitchen, we passed a window on the outside, placed our cup in the window and received one small ladle of soup in our cup. We ate and then went around the kitchen building and back up to our building. It was night. Building No. 42 had only two small lights each placed about one third of the way down the aisle from each end of the building. I could hardly see, the light was so bad.

With all the inconvenience placed before us, there is still no way I can even began to tell you how good it felt, or how grateful I was the Lord had seen fit to let me survive and make it thus far. My feet looked like pieces of raw meat, blistered and bleeding. But the straw mattress and bed was a blessing after so long without a place to lie down except frozen ground and snow and slippery wet foxholes. That night when I finally lay down on the hard lumpy straw mattress, it felt so good. It was mine and it was dry. I don't think I could have slept any better had I been on a feather bed with linen sheets and pillow!

But! (When the word but comes up, something always comes out and believe me it did). That gourmet soup I had for supper had to have a new home and I obliged. It must have been around three or four in the morning, I tried to make it to the slit trench (toilet) out behind the building. I made it. On my way back, as I walked down the aisle towards my bed, I did something I thought I would never get over. I stole me a pair of boots. Or did I? (You be the judge.)

As you know I had no boots from the time I awoke in the German aid station and was taken prisoner of war. You had to have seen my feet to believe the condition they were in. As I walked down the aisle, about midway the building, I stumbled and fell flat on my face over a pair of boots. I picked them up, looked at them and got up off the floor. I looked around to see if I had disturbed anyone but it seemed everyone was enjoying their bed for the first time in weeks. No one moved. I sat back down with the boots still in my hand. Thinking back, I realized no one in the building knew me; I sure did not know any of them. As far as I could tell, no one else knew I did not have any boots.

I stumbled over the boots fairly close to one of the two small lights. The boots appeared to be my size. I made up my mind then and there to keep that pair of boots.

Now! I could sit here and write one excuse after another, explaining about my feet. How sore they were, as to why, I took the boots. But this does not alter the fact. If you knowingly take something which does not belong to you, it's stealing. I went back to bed feeling I had stolen the boots. I could not sleep the rest of the night.

At break of day, we were roused out of the building for a head count. The guards came up with one man missing. They counted again. Still one man missing. They counted twice more. Each time they were short a man. We stood in formation as the guards went into the building to try and locate the missing man.

Shortly they returned. They stated the man was dead in his bed.

Before returning to our building the guards marched us down to the kitchen for morning coffee. (That's what they called it.) I don't know what it was! But, it was hot and that is what counted.

When we returned to the building, the dead man was still in bed, where he stayed most of the day. Our group was new in camp and we did not know what to do with the dead soldier. Finally, one of the guards came around and had us to move him to an empty room in building No.43.

I was appointed to the dead man moving. While moving him, I realized the boots belonged to him. But no one ever mentioned anything about any boots of shoes I learned later when a man died his boots were removed anyway.

No one knew I had taken the man's boots except God and me. I felt I had stolen those boots for a selfish reason. For a long time I talked to the Lord about what I had done without any satisfaction. Then one day when I was talking with the Lord about the boots, I asked if he had placed those boots at the right place at the right time. I asked if he wanted me to have them would he please remove this guilty feeling from me. To this day, I never new if the man was dead when I got the boots. But I do know this: From the day I prayed, unless an occasion arises that I am reminded of it, I never think about those boots and I have never felt like I stole them any more.

I fully believe God intended for me to have those boots.

What do you think? Did I steal them or did God give them to me?

By the way, they were just my size.

After we squared the dead man away in building No.43, it must have been about nine a.m., all of us from building No.42 was called out. We were put into formation by the guards and marched across the camp to the interrogation building. Each one of us was interviewed. They asked what outfits we were in and who was our commanding officer? They asked how long had we been in combat, where were we from in the states.

They asked me all kind of questions about the outfit I was in. But all they got from me was my name, rank, and serial number. After the interrogation we were issued German ID tags with numbers. The German officer who interrogated me spoke very good English and appeared to appeared to be a complete gentleman.

The whole interrogation lasted about an hour. When the Officer finished questioning me, he had me put outside in the cold in a barbwire compound with several others. All the men had remained outside until each man was interrogated. Afterwards, we all returned back to building No.42. Somewhere around five or five thirty p.m., it was head count time, and then down to the kitchen for a half of cup of something called soup. Then back to our quarters.

That just about covers the first day in the Prisoner of War camp.

The next day I sought information about medical care. No one seemed to know anything about a doctor in the P.O.W. camp. I learned several days later that a doctor was in fact in the camp and located in a certain building. I sought treatment for my eye. When I got there, the doctor said all he had was some cleaning material. He did not know if he could get anymore. He said he would wash and keep my eye clean the best he could. If I came in from time to time.

Finally, my eye began to get well. (When your eye meets the butt of a rifle, it doesn't get well overnight.)

As we begin to settle down into camp life, everything seemed pretty much routine: formations, headcount, morning coffee and evening soup, then back to quarters. Sometimes we were selected for a detail. Almost every morning there was a body to bury. The burial was always outside the camp. In the wooded area, we dug graves and placed the bodies, covering them with leaves and some straw before throwing the dirt over them.

Then there were wood details. The details went into the woods with the guards and gathered wood for the heaters in the buildings. We had to carry the wood in our arms or on our backs to camp. There was one detail that is not easy to talk about. I won't ever get it out of my mind. It lives with me day and night. It's been with me for over sixty years and I know it will remain with me the rest of my life. I am in my eighty's as I write this and I know it will be with me to the end. And the one thing which keeps me going, is the scripture found in *Revelation 21: 3-4.*

"God himself will wipe away all tears from our eyes and there shall be no more death, nor sorrow, nor crying or pain, all of that will be gone forever."

I look forward to this relief some day. The detail I'm referring to was when you go into the camp, where the Germans destroyed the Jews. Your whole insides just about come out. You see the gas chambers where thousands of people like you and me were led to thinking they were going to get showers, only to have the doors locked.

And instead of water coming out of the shower heads it was gas.

The bodies were then taken out of the chambers and thrown in ditches and trenches covered by dirt pushing bulldozers. What really got my attention in a bad way was the building where lots of bodies were burned.

The end of the long red brick building was opened and closed by huge fire doors. Down the middle of the building was a set of tracks (like small rail road tracks) only smaller. The tracks carried flatbed cars like rail cars. These cars were loaded with dead bodies and pulled down the tracks by a cable. The building was no longer just a building. It was a furnace. When the rail cars passed through the flames, the bodies were burned. At the other end of the building (furnace) the bodies that did not burn had to be removed and placed in the ditches or trench. Bodies were again loaded on the cars and sent back through the furnace, being disposed of at both ends of the building.

As I walked to one side of the compound I faced a field looked to be somewhere around two acres of land. There was a solid fence around it. More like a square box. Around the walls on three sides, were cubicles, like phone booths and the other wall of the square was a control area for training dogs. These booths were about five foot apart with the front of the booth open. These were the booths used to train dogs.

The Germans would stand a Jew prisoner in each booth and from the control center send out dogs to a certain booth to kill the one in the booth. They continued until the dog was trained to do what it was told to do: kill the prisoner as directed.

I did not see any of the killings, but I sure saw the results. These are events you try to keep silent about, especially if you have had every human right taken away from you, being forced to live like an animal. There is no way anyone can describe how it feels to have no human rights whatsoever; unless you were there. And I was, after living like an animal, month after month, you almost become one.

As the months passed in the camp, spring came and weeds and grass came up. I was so hungry by then. By this time, the Germans had no food for themselves, so there was no way they were going to give any to POW's. There was no more soup. Only black bread.

To start with we had gotten one loaf of bread at night, to be divided between four men. This was all the food we got each day. This lasted for about two weeks. The bread ration was cut six men per day.

One week later, the bread was cut to eight men per day, then ten men per day. Finally, the last month we were in camp the bread was cut to twelve men per day. There was one week that the Germans ran out of bread and we got two small potatoes, (about one and half to two inches in diameter), each day. That was all.

Now Stalag 9B, (our POW camp) was different from the other camps. We were more like a holding camp. Most all the POW's from generals to privates passed through 9B, and then they were shipped to different camps. Stalag 9B was not a working camp. We had some details but nothing like the work camps. And since we were not a working camp, we got less food than any of the camps.

Medical care was something you read about. There were never any medical supplies and Red Cross package? We didn't even know what they looked like. Each morning we still got the hot water they called coffee. I must say here, had I not eaten weeds, grass, roots and bark off trees I would not have survived.

My friend, you talk about being hungry! When you watch your flesh roll off your body, like sweat rolling off your forehead, you know what hungry is. When I was first taken prisoner, my weight was 188 pounds. When I came out of that place, my weight was 93 pounds. There was not enough meat on my tail to sit without bruising.

When the food began to run out and one loaf of bread had to be divided into twelve portions, every little crumb counted to each man. We had no way to equally divide the loaf. When you are starving and you don't get your fair share, you can imagine what friction it caused.

At the beginning of the "bread only" we faced a problem dividing the bread. Sometimes, prior to this, I was working on a detail breaking small rocks using claw hammers. The crushed rock was used to go into walkways. Well, while working one day, I found a piece of metal barrel hoop about six inches long. Luckily, the end of the hoop was the end where the rivets fastened the hoop together. The old rivets were out leaving holes in the metal.

Now, I took the metal and made a knife so we could divide the bread equally. I still have the knife, and spoon I made out of a limb. I smoothed the spoon by rubbing it with small rocks. I know you are wondering what in the world would I be doing with a spoon if we no longer had soup. My friend, "preparation, faith, and hope!" Without it, you come up on the short side.

I never got to use the spoon but I had it just in case.

If you happen to visit the Veterans Hospital in Atlanta, Georgia, there is a wall in the hospital they call the POW wall. The hospital honored us POW's by displaying our pictures on this wall. Mine is there along with a picture of my knife and spoon. you might like to visit with us while you are there. The knife proved to be a life saver as each man got his fair share of the loaf of bread.

Each man in the group would take a turn dividing the loaf of bread. It was the rule agreed on by the group, that whoever divided the loaf, would always get the last piece.

I suppose by now you are wondering, what about clothes? Well all we had is what we had on. And when the weather warmed up I took a water hose and washed my clothes the best I could by turning the hose on myself while still in them. This worked for a little while, but I had to stop doing this because the water pressure tore holes in my clothes. The clothes were just too old and worn out. I wore the same clothes for over 180 days! Can you imagine? (No, You can't imagine just how it was, and you can count that a blessing.)

Things got really bad with me those last days in the P.O.W. camp. In the morning we were called out a short time after daybreak, for headcount. Then we had to stand in line over an hour to get the morning coffee, being sick with stomach problems from eating weeds, grass; and anything I could find. I was weak for the lack of food. Snow was up to my knees, with no heavy coat on and one pair of pants (full of holes). As I stood there, cold, wet hungry and sick, I prayed for God to take me out of it all.

At night I had started praying for God to take me before I had to face another day. I'd wake up in the morning to face the same misery as the day before. During the brutally cold nights-- not having any heat in the building to speak of--and with only one blanket per man, we doubled up to keep from freezing. The man on the top bunk would drop down with his blanket and sleep with the man in the third bed. I slept with the man in the first bed with my blanket. With two men sleeping in a two foot bed, there was not much room, but we stayed warmer. We survived.

One night, around midnight, the guards came into the building with weapons. They rushed everybody out into the cold and snow and lined us up by the building. They trained a machine gun on us and made us stand there until almost daylight. We did not know if we were going to be shot, but we fully expected to be shot for they had us looking down the barrel of that machine gun for all those hours. It was terror.

Just before daylight, we were returned to our bunks, still not knowing what was happening. When we got back into the building, every bed had been torn apart. We learned later, a crew had gone through our building searching for bread. Seemed some men had gone to the kitchen and attacked the cook with a hatchet. They didn't kill him although he was very badly injured. But they did steal some bread.

The guards claimed they found the ones who did it. I don't know who or how many was in on the deal. And within the hour, we were back in formation for head count, and coffee.

Each day we tried to quote some scripture. We had no Bible and the only song we could sing was, "*I Come to the Garden Alone.*" If you have ever felt the spirit of the Lord, you will understand what I'm saying. When you see a building full of POW's, some of them too weak from starvation to stand, sitting and lying on the floor trying to sing, you see faith. We continuously asked God to help us survive by helping our brothers in arms out on the front lines bring the war to an end so we could return home to our loved ones. We begged God to give us strength to survive. Some of the men cried, some prayed and some just sat and gazed into space.

Those pictures I have never forgotten.

In early April 1945, in the stillness of the night, we heard big artillery guns. At first we were worried, for it was known that when Germans were forced to withdraw or run, they moved in the direction of a POW Camp, hoping to draw fire from our allied forces. In cases where this could not be done, the Germans bypassed the POW camp and stopped. Then they set up artillery guns and lobbed shells back into the POW camp.

This was just another problem added to our many. At any rate that night we heard the guns. The closer they got to us, the louder they became. Finally, we could hear small arms weapons fire. We knew allied forces were close. In fact, the small armed weapons were getting so close that night we could see tracer rounds being fired.

One morning we woke up and no guards and no German personnel of any kind could be found. We expected the Germans to try and level the camp with artillery shells. That did not happen and later we learned why. General Patton and his tanks had kept the Germans on the run so fast, the Germans did not have the time to set up their artillery and fire back.

Then reality hit. We knew our troops were not far away and would get to us soon.

We knew we were fixing to be set free.

As I write this I find myself standing inside the barbed wire fence looking out. It's been well over 65 years ago (like yesterday) watching American tank's tear holes in the prison walls, leaving gaps large enough to drive a trucks through.

Shortly after sunrise on that blessed day of liberation, the trucks loaded with C-rations came through the gaps. Two men stood on the trucks throwing cases of rations off on each side of the truck. When the cases hit the ground they'd burst and cans of food flew in all directions. If you have ever lived on a farm where there were pigs in a pen and you took a bag of corn on the cob to feed them throwing maybe four or five ears into the pen and you know how pigs act. If there are a dozen pigs in a pen, each one of them will try to get to the corn, doing whatever it takes. Unless you have seen it, or went through it, you would not believe human beings would act like animals. But we did.

In fact that morning we acted worse than animals. All we could think of was trying to survive. It's like being on the battle field you have a gun and the enemy has a gun. You don't stand in a foxhole or lay on the ground and wonder. Should I or should I not? You survive. You shoot. You act on instinct.

My friend as surely as I'm sitting here writing, I tell you the truth. It is easier to try to survive on the battle field facing gun than trying to survive from hunger.

Tell you what! Suppose you pick eleven people along with yourself, knowing they love to eat as well as you do. Knowing the only food you can look forward to (for the twelve of you) is one loaf of black bread mixed with sawdust approximately eight inches long, four inches deep and five inches wide to be shared. One loaf a day, week after week which turns into months after months. Throw in being beat and humiliated, stripped of every human right you ever had, being treated worse than an animal. Is it any wonder you don't act like an animal?

That morning I got a can of corned beef hash. I started eating and found my stomach had closed up so much I could not eat but a very little at a time. One can last me all day.

I stood by the fence watching men go out through the holes. Most everyone who was going out, stopped and raised his hands towards heaven, then took a long deep breaths, not once, but several times. They breathed the fresh air of freedom, and then turned and walked slowly away.

I watched with tears on my face and thought, well that's that. This is done with. The days of waiting are over. Now what? I thought now that, at the end of the seventh day, the resting is finished. We begin a new day of a new week of a new life. We're out of the womb of stagnancy. We're out of the tomb of exile. We're Free! Time takes a sharper cadence. The seconds and minutes shine with newness which stuns the eyes.

But the shoulders are hunched and the foot steps are slow.

It took a little while for me to get reacquainted with Miss Freedom which I had not seen in 180 days.

The Freedom Walk

We POW's walked out of the camp and four miles down the mountain to Bad Orb, Germany joining with our advance troops who were already there. We had our first real meal. Military Police -- called M.P.'s-- drove through Bad Orb announcing over loud speakers that trucks were being provided to take all POW's back up the hill to camp. They told us to return at once, for they had already begun flying POW's to France to the medical center called Lucky Strike.

The trucks were located at the foot of the hill. General Patton was supplying gas for his tanks, delivered in five gallon containers and flown in on C-47 planes They reloaded these C-47's with POW's and flew us to Lucky Strike.

I had to fly out the next day, because when the truck from Bad Orb got me back to camp, the last plane had already left for the day.

Early next morning, trucks transported some of us to the aid field where the planes landed again to unload the gas containers. There were no seats or benches in the plane in order to accommodate the gas cans. We sat and lay down in the plane for the trip to France. When we landed at the airport near Lucky Strike medical center, we were met by trucks with pillows to sit on. There wasn't enough meat on our tails to keep from bruising while being transported.

The hospital had set up tents. We went into one of the tents and removed all our clothes, discarding them in a container. The next tent was the shower tent, and was attached and divided by a drop curtain. OH BOY, something we had not had for many long months! After a good long shower, we moved through the curtain into another tent and got sprayed with delousing powder. Next tent, we picked up underwear, pants, shirt, and boots. After getting fitted and dressed, we went to the mess hall for something, we had not though existed any more. Food! While we were eating, the Mess Sergeant tapped on one of the tables.

He said he had an order from the hospital commander. The order stated that POW's coming to the kitchen would be fed regardless of the time of day or night.

The Mess Sergeant said, "And I want to add this. Not only will you be fed, I will see to it you get what you want if we have it in the kitchen!" He got a standing ovation. After the meal, we were taken to a hospital ward and assigned a bed.

That night, I slept in a bed with clean sheets, a pillow with pillow case and breathed the fresh air of freedom. Needless to say, oh, how I slept. Next morning I got out of bed and went to the mess hall. One of the cooks asked me what I wanted to eat.

I said "If you have it, I would like a couple of eggs over light with grits and a slab of ham with toast."

He said, "Partner if you hang loose for a couple of minutes, you'll have it."

Shortly, my breakfast was ready and what a great breakfast it was. I could not eat all of it because my stomach wouldn't let me. After breakfast, I returned to the hospital ward, slipped off my boots and stretched out on my bed hopping to be called for my physical.

Finally, my name was called over the loud speaker. I asked the ward master if he knew what was going on. He said they were calling for those to be loaded on a truck taken to the air port and flown back to the states. He reminded me I had not had my medical check-up yet and could not go. I looked at him and said." Watch me!"

I got up and slipped on my boots. As I turned to walk out, the Sergeant said "I've not heard a word you have said, and I sure haven't seen you go, but good luck partner."

I walked outside and answered to my name. And loaded on the truck. Before the day was out, I was on my way back to the United States of America! We landed at an airport in New Jersey and were taken by bus to Camp Kilmer.

We were then taken to the post theater where we were moved inside so the Post Commander could welcome us back home. Shortly afterwards, the Post Commander came out on stage. He looked at us. For a long time.

Finally he said, "Well! I guess you men have heard I was going to give you men a fifteen day furlough? Well I'm not." He sounded as serious as a heart attack. I looked around. No one smiled. Then the Commander added, "I'm not even going to give you ten days." By then lines of disappointment had every face in the theater warped out of shape.

He said "I'm not even going to give you five days." Seeing the look on our faces, he added very quickly, "I'm giving you thirty days leave! Welcome home men, good to have you back with us."

How quickly the expressing on our faces changed. He gave us a very warn welcome home speech. Afterwards, he said we would leave the theater and go to lunch and at 1300 hours which was 1:00 p.m., processing would begin. We would receive some of our pay. We were also issued orders telling us where to report to after our leave was up.

Home

After processing was over, we were free to go home any way we chose at our own expense. It was late in the evening and we were invited to spend the night if we wanted to. Arrangements had been made for us just in case. Some of us stayed until the next day so we could get clothing fit to wear home. My clothes were the ones issued me back at Camp Lucky Strike in France. (Remember I had left the medical center before my physical with the clothes I had received after the shower) The shirt had several holes in it.

When I asked about the holes, I was told by the Sergeant who issued it, to me, "These clothes are used clothes belonging to troops who came to the hospital for treatment and didn't need them any more. In fact they don't need any clothes ever. Those are bullet holes." I sure didn't want to go home with bullet holes in my shirt!

After receiving another outfit the next day (and after another good breakfast) I left for home.

As I was waiting at the bus stop, the Sergeant who had eaten breakfast with me came by and asked me where I was gong?

"To Douglas, Georgia," I said.

He asked, "How are you going? "

"By bus I think," I said.

"Oh you don't want to go by bus. Takes to long, I'm going to Montgomery, Alabama. Come with me and I'll show you how to beat the bus by hours."

That sounded good to me, I said. So the Sergeant and I left Camp Kilmer hitch-hiking. The first ride we got was with a man driving a semi-truck, loaded with meat, going to Atlanta, Georgia. We got into Atlanta early in the morning and stopping at another truck stop so the man could fuel up.

There I caught another truck to Albany, Georgia. The Sergeant was able to catch a truck into Montgomery.

We said good bye and was on our separate ways.

Finally, I arrived home. That was a day I had thought I would never see again. It was a day I had hoped and prayed for so many times. I don't believe I have ever been as happy as I was then.

The thing I cherished most was the fact God had protected and kept me safe through all the terrifying times I endured. I have no doubt in my mind, without God's intervention in my life I would not be sitting here writing this book. My wish is in the years to come, these words I have penned will be read and folks will remember the price so many of us paid for the freedom of our country.

I learned many years ago, all that God asks of us is to believe when we ask him for help and protection. He will supply our needs. How well I know this to be true. When you have given everything except your life, (which God gave you), you will remember where it all came from. Sometimes it takes that to get our attention. It is my prayer you want ever get to that point before realizing God is God, and the Lord Jesus is the only hope we have.

Things moved pretty fast for me after I was liberated from the POW camp. In a little over a month I was home and married! On arriving home I didn't go to my parent's house for a couple of days. I went to my girl's house. We had to make plans for our wedding.

It was in the middle of the week, so I decided I would not go to my parent's until the weekend. We lived in the country, and everyone in the country would go to town (Douglas, Georgia) on Saturday.

Now Douglas was a small town. Its main street covered about all the shopping area there was. I knew my mom and dad would be in town on Saturday. I knew it would be no problem finding them.

Sure enough, on Saturday I walked up the street and saw my mom walking in the same direction I was some thirty or forty feet in front of me. I very quickly slipped up behind her and put my hands over her eyes, I held her that way a few seconds. When I released her, Oh Boy!

She wheeled around seeing me and the first thing she said, "I should just whip you!" See, my mother had no idea I was out of the POW camp, let alone home. My mom had nerves of steel. She had five sons out of six in the service of our country during wars in Germany, Korea and Viet Nam.

It sure was so good being back with my family. But one of the hardest things facing me was trying to adjust being human again. (Remember when you live like an animal, you almost become one.) Even now, some 65 years later my daily life is spent walking on egg shells. I have to watch everything I say and do. The scars will always be there. There is no going to bed at night with a completely clear mind. No good night's sleep. At times I dread seeing night come.

It is 5:23 a.m. as I write this and I've been writing since 2:09 a.m. waiting for daylight to come. The older you get the longer the nights are. At times you have to get out of bed in order to get relief and clear your mind of the awful things happened in combat 65 years ago.

War is awful. When you are involved in war you always feel the results of it. Most nights seems like yesterday. Without the help of the Lord, I could not survive even now.

Mildred and I were married while I was home on leave. After my 30 day leave, my orders were to report to Miami Beach, Florida for rehabilitation. The military had hotels on the beach where men returning from combat could go for retreat. I was assigned to Berkeley Shore Hotel. On arrival to the hotel, I reported to the Commanding Officer. He welcomed and thanked me for what I endured as a POW, and for my service to our country.

He asked, "Didn't you just get married?"

"Yes, sir," I said.

"Your wife is at home?" he added.

"Right again, sir."

"I have assigned you to a private room, so why don't you get your wife down here and have a honeymoon on the Army?" he Said.

"Sounds good to me sir."

He said, "You're going to be here a while anyway."

And he was not kidding. It was over six months before I received an assignment.

Mildred and I had a wonderful honeymoon. In Fact we had four weeks of it.

I was then informed by the Commanding Officer that a hurricane was expected to hit the beach and it would be best if I sent my wife home for safety reasons. So you know the old saying, the honeymoon was over!

When I got my new assignment it was to Oliver General Hospital in Augusta, Georgia, as a patient. Several months later I was assigned to the hospital posting medical records. I became a soldier again and remained at the hospital until it closed. At that time, the hospital personnel were then assigned to Camp Gordon, which was also located in Augusta, Georgia.

All this was in 1946.

Old Soldiers Never Die

In 1950, I was selected along with 15 other men from different camps of the U.S. Army. And from other states, who met for the first time on the docks in San Francisco. California. Let's step back for just a moment and see how and why we were meeting on the docks in

California at that day and time.

Each man had started the assignment thinking he was on his own only to find, on arrival he was part of a special group being loaded on a civilian ship, and sent to Japan to work for General Douglas MacArthur in the General Head Quarters (GHQ).

I learned later, each man had been selected in the same way I was. This being, one Monday morning I was asked by the First Sergeant to join him in his office. On arrival, he handed me a sheet of paper with instructions as to where to go and what building and room to report to. In doing so he said "NO QUESTIONS! You will know what to do when you get to the appointed place.

I looked the instruction sheet. I had to report no later than 10:00 a.m. that day. I had one half hour to get to the appointed place. I said, "Okay, Sergeant," and left.

When I arrived there were ten other men sitting at desks taking a test. The instructor handed me a pamphlet with instructions and said I had two hours to complete it.

It didn't take long to find out what the other ten men were doing. When the two hours were up, the instructor picked up the papers, dismissed the group for lunch with instructions to be back in our seat by two o'clock p.m. for another two hour test. After we completed the last test, which ended at four o'clock p.m. we were told our First Sergeant would notify each one of us what to do next.

He said no questions would be answered, and good-by.

Two days later, the First Sergeant called me into his office. He said, "Pack your bags. You are on your way to California. He handed me a plane ticket on a flight out of Augusta Georgia. He informed me that my flight would be leaving at 9:00 o'clock on the following Monday. I had been selected from testing for a job in General Headquarters in Japan.

And that's how the group met on the dock on that day.

When I arrived at the airport there was a military vehicle waiting for me. When the plane landed, the driver asked me my name, rank and serial number. I responded and was told to get into the car. On the way from the airport to the California docks the driver never said a word. I tried several times to get him in a conversation, without any respond. I could not even get a good old grunt out of him.

Now friend, this old country boy began to sit up and take notice. I let my mind race back over the last few days trying to figure out just what had happened. It seems everyone I talked to about what was taking place had eternal lockjaw. Well, curiosity was jumping all over this old boy. As I sat there in the back seat of the vehicle on my way to Lord knows where, the driver kept looking at me in the rearview mirror. When he saw me looking at him, he quickly turned his eyes to the road. Yep, you know how it is when old ugly thoughts began to slip into your mind. Mine was double timing. At this stage of whatever game the driver had going, I could not keep from smiling a little. I told myself, J.D. If you had a good bowl of beans for supper, you could have gassed the old boy about now. Wonder what kind of response I would get from him then? I concluded he would just have rolled the window down, and kept on driving.

Finally we arrived at the docks. The driver pointed at a group of soldiers, informing me I was to join them and wait, as an Officer would be joining us shortly. The shortly turned out to be two hours. In the meantime the 16 of us got to know each other pretty well. We learned we all went through the same routine with the testing and now this arrival. While standing around mumbling, with our hands in our pocket up to our elbows (something a soldier should never do.) Our fearless leader, the officer, finally arrived.

Oh Boy! The expression on his face! It wasn't hard to figure out what he was thinking with the attitude he had. (Mothers have all kinds of boys, you know.)

Among the 16 of us, relaxation slipped away our hands came out of pockets. The first thing the officer said, "SERGEANT

LANKFORD?" I didn't respond. I just presented myself to him in a military manner. He handed me a roster of the 16 men along with tickets covering us for the trip to Japan aboard the civilian ship. He said, "You are the ranking man in the group. It is your responsibility to see these men get to Japan on this ship. Get your men and follow me. I will take you aboard and show you to your quarters."

I assembled my men and went aboard. The officer showed us our quarters on "C" deck and to my surprise we were assigned two men per room. All rooms were on the same side of the hall and I hardly believe my eyes. After all, this was a commercial Ship loaded with civilians.

Friend, you talk about sure-nough up town. Why, I would've had to sell a couple of hogs and at least a cow or two, to have afforded even one night in a room like that. And all of the rooms were the same.

After I assigned the men their rooms with instructions to remain there until further notice, the officer asked me to follow him. He wanted to introduce me to the head servant of the deck. The servant would be working with me in regards to ship regulations and procedures. The officer told the servant he should work with me on any problem or occasion, which may arise in regards to the soldiers. The servant agreed and said he would get me all schedules, events, programs and the need-to-know procedures for me and would have them at my room within an hour.

We thanked him and left. I arrived back at my quarters. The officer never did introduce himself but said he would like to speak with me privately. I sent the man in the room with me out, asking him to give us a few moments alone.

The officer said "The ship is going to stop over in Hawaii for three days and nights to unload and reload supplies and passengers. You are the ranking man among this group, therefore you understand you are in charge and will be held accountable for these men until they reach their destination. When the Ship docks in Hawaii, Passengers will go ashore. As for the men going ashore, that's up to you. I suggest you keep in mind you are responsible for them.

"Any questions?"

"No, sir."

"Have a good trip" and left. For good I should add because I Never knew his name! I never saw him again.

Shortly after the procedures, schedules, and need-to-know information was delivered to me, I had my roommate assemble the men in the relaxation room for a meeting at 3 o'clock p.m. (only half hour away) I went over the material the servant had sent to me so I would know how and what to explain to the men.

At the meeting, I covered the material I had on ship procedures, making sure each one understood them. During the discussion I didn't tell the men about the layover in Hawaii. I wanted them to have a clear understanding of what was expected of each one of them. The meeting ended, with instructions for them to stand by for supper. We had missed lunch and we were ready to eat. I suggested we all go to the dining room together, until we learned how things operated. I explained that it might be we found eating as a group each meal would be better for all. We just don't know at this time what to do or expect. We would go as a group and see what happened. At suppertime, the men and I arrived at the dinning room on time according to schedule.

A male waiter met us at the door. This fellow had one of them white towels hanging over his arm and a bow tie on. You talk about first class, Oh Boy! I led the pack. He came straight to me, no smile, no greeting, and no nothing.

"Follow me" was his remark and he was off. He led us to the back corner of the main dining room. The section was already occupied with 17 soldiers; only these soldiers were females (WACS)! The dining section was small so we had to share tables. I was asked by their Sergeant would I share the table with her.

It would be an honor," I replied. During the meal we discussed how we all had gotten where we were.

She said she and her crew were selected through testing just as we had been. She asked me if I had any idea what was coming off. "No," I told her. "All I was told was we had a job to do at GHQ."

She said, "That's all I could get out of anyone. Were you informed about the layover in Hawaii?"

"Yes"

"Have you told your men yet?

"No," I said.

"I've not told my girls either. Frankly, I don't know what to do. Are you going to let your men go ashore?"

"Yep. After I lay down some hard rules that will be complied with."

"Will you work with me and see if you and I can come up with some kind of plan so I can let my girls go?"

"Yes, if you can control your girls."

"That I can and will do."

"We will see," I said and smiled.

The Sergeant and I met in the relaxation room to figure out how we could let our troops go ashore together and feel safe about it. She was worried about her girls being out by themselves. She didn't want to order them to remain in groups of four, for protection and safety reasons. I thought of a plan that would work if accepted by her. I didn't mention it. I wanted to see if she was thinking along the same line I was. I felt pretty sure she was, but I remained quiet.

Finally, she asked me what I thought of letting one man and one woman go together in a group of two couples. That way, each girl would feel safe having a man with her. I could not tell her I had already thought of it. In my judgment, that was about the only way to go.

My reply was. "You mean, pair them off?"

"Why, yes. What do you think?"

"You might have something there. You understand if we agree to do this, there will be rules and regulations which must be honored by all. Let me say here and now, so there will be no misunderstanding. Any soldier, when I look at this group I don't see Men and women, I see soldiers, failing to comply with rules and orders we issue, and if the offense requires punishment, the soldier will be placed in confinement until we reach our destination. There he, she, or they will be tried under article 31 of the military code of conduct. Sergeant! you have a choice. Either we are together on this or we are not. As far as my men, they will comply. They will go ashore and conduct themselves as soldiers and gentlemen. And, I will do my very best to see they enjoy what little time they have before heading into, Lord knows what. The decision is yours. Either my men go alone, or they will escort your girls."

"I concur completely," she said. "Now, how do we pair them off?"

"Good lady, "I said, I think we should let them pair themselves off. You and I should have a meeting with them, letting them know about the layover, and that we've decided to let them go ashore while we're there, only under certain conditions. We will then have another meeting explaining what is expected."

She smiled in agreement.

"I don't know how long it'll take to get to Hawaii. I've not received that information yet. I suggest we tell them about the buddy system you suggested, about going ashore. Man-Woman so they'll have time to get to know each other and prepare. In the meantime you and I should start working on the conditions."

The Sergeant and I had a meeting with her troops, informing them of the layover. We told them we all would be going ashore under certain conditions."

"We have not worked out all of the details yet," I explained. Sergeant Roberson will let you in on a couple of them for your consideration and approval.

"If you girls go ashore you will go as a group, and remain so each time you go. I'll take you myself. The other option we have, and for your consideration and approval, I suggested to Sergeant Lankford and he had agreed, to ask his men to escort the girl's one man, one woman, going only in groups of two couples. He and I feel this would be a safe way for all of us so we can enjoy the time we have."

The girls smiled, but didn't say anything. I said, "The choice is up to you girls. I've not told my men anything about this. I don't think you girls will have any problem getting an escort. The Sergeant said we would let you know about a couple of conditions. She explained you had two options. If you chose the first option, so be it. You and your sergeant will be on your own. If you choose the latter, using my men as escorts, you will become a group of military personal as a whole, therefore even your sergeant will have a boss and you are looking at him. You soldiers know the ranking person in a group of military personnel is in charge. I suggest *very strongly* that you don't forget this."

The Sergeant had already explained one of the two conditions she and I agreed on. I'm going to use this word again. If and that's IF, we go ashore, you will return to the ship for roll call at a time yet to be decided. Along with the entire do's, don'ts, will, won't, can and cant's, which we will give you at another meeting before we reach Hawaii."

I continued, "Any soldier failing to return to the ship when ordered, will be considered "AWOL," (absent with out leave) and tried under article 31 of the military code of conduct on arrival at our destination.

"Ladies and gentleman, I use this term for I expect nothing less from each one of you. You and I have a chance of a lifetime, which probably won't ever come again, to visit Hawaii. We will have three days so, let's make the best if it. Only if we try, we can make these three days something we can cherish the rest of our lives. When we leave here, we are heading into a war zone and if you haven't thought about it already, let me remind you. We will not playing ring around the roses when we get there."

Sergeant Roberson nodded.

I continued, "War is pure hell. All you know about war is what you have been told by a friend or seen in the movies. I've been there. So I know what I'm talking about. I was in four major conflicts earning four Bronze Battle Stars in the Battle of the Bugle with the 106th Infantry Division. I was a Prisoner of War and dropped weight from 188 pounds to 93. I've eaten grass, weeds, bark off trees, roots, most anything I could get my hands on to survive. So don't even think about taking where we are going lightly. And, we have no idea what we will be doing. But there's one thing you and I do know. We have been singled out as a special group, placed on a commercial ship going to be docked in Hawaii for three days. Lets be what we are, ladies, gentlemen and soldiers. Sergeant Roberson and I will do everything we can to see you have a good visit."

The meeting ended. As the troops left the room you could see the joyful smiles on the WACS's faces as they chatted with each other.

I wish I could say as much for myself as I left the meeting. I made it a point to be the last one to leave the room. My heart was very heavy. I was sad, for I knew those young soldiers could not even imagine how bad war was. Where there's war lives will be lost. I felt in my bones, some of them would never make it back home a live. And some didn't.

The last night before reaching Hawaii, we had our final meeting. And what a joy it was watching those troops acting like kids the night before Christmas.

The next morning, when it was cleared to go ashore, the Sergeant and I stood at the gangplank and watched the troops move off of the ship in couples. They were so excited and happy. I could not keep from wondering what to expect for letting them go ashore. I turned to the Sergeant and ask how she felt about the situation?

She looked at me and smiled "You're worried, aren't you?"

"Not really," I said.

"Well, don't be. I've talked with my girls, and I know you have done the same with your men. They will be all right, let's go ashore and enjoy the sights."

Each day became more joyful to those troops. And Sergeant Robertson was right, I've never seen a group of complete strangers, with nothing in the world to tie them together except their uniforms, get along and respected each other as those troops did. Those three days planted seeds of good memories in the heart and minds of all 33 of us. If any conflict occurred among any of them, it was never known by myself or the other Sergeant. So yes, we had our vacation. And we put more into those three days than you would normally cover in a week on a regular vacation. I won't even try to explain what all we did and saw while ashore. All I know and I'm speaking for the rest of the gang, is that it was just wonderful. And the only thing I regret was I failed to keep a roster of my men. Also one of Sergeant Roberson and her troops.

There is a bond in the military which draws soldiers together. A bond of respect and trust. Each one knows there are times when your life is in the other's hands, especially in combat. In order to perform as you must, the trust must be there. When we left Hawaii for Japan, little did we know just how soon some of us would be relying on that bond of trust.

The next day, while out at sea we ran into a storm, and boy, did we have some sick soldiers!

I don't think some of them ate anything for a couple of days.

Sergeant Roberson asked if I knew anything about laundry facilities aboard. I didn't know a thing, but right after dinner I saw one of the servants at a distance. He had his back toward me. After I got his attention and he turned around I saw it was the old sourpuss who had directed us to our first meal. Had I known who it was I would not have contacted him.

But when I asked about the laundry, not only did he take me to the laundry room, he set the machines so we could use them without having to put in coins. He suggested it would be best if we did our laundry at night. He said he would reset the machines in the morning, but would set them for us at night! He did everything he could to make our trip joyful and comfortable.

He was so nice to us I was compelled to apologize to him for the opinion I initially had of him. The man just smiled and said "don't even think about it sergeant. With the face I have it happens all the time!"

I felt so ashamed. The man shook my hand, turned and walked away. As I watched him go. I thought only of one scripture: *Judge not, and ye shall not be judged: condemn not, and ye shall not be condemned: forgive, and ye shall be forgiven: Luke. 6:37.*

We arrived in Yokohama. Japan, early one morning. After breakfast, I prepared the men to go ashore. In less than an hour my men and I were standing, along with Sergeant Roberson and her girls, on the dock awaiting transportation. In less than a half hour, two military trucks pulled up. We were a little disappointed to being put on trucks instead of a bus for the trip to GHQ.

When the trucks stopped, an officer got out of each truck. One came to me and my men. The other officer approached Sergeant Roberson and her girls. The officer approached me, called me by name. "Where are your orders?" He asked.

What orders! The only thing given to me back in California was a roster of the men, with verbal orders to see that they got to Japan.

The officer asked. "Are all of the men here?

"Yes, sir, here's the roster. Want a roll call?" I said.

"No I'll take your word for it. Take your men aboard the truck. It will take you were you need to go. On arrival, someone will meet you and you will be instructed as to what to do and where to go from there".

We loaded one truck and the girls loaded the other. We yelled back and forth, "see you over at GHQ". We waved to each other.

Little did any of us know the chattering, fellowship, and goodbye waves would be the last time we ever saw those girls again.

The truck carried us to a supply building where we were issued full combat gear and equipment. And, before the sun went down that day me and my 15 men with me were loaded aboard a small boat and sent directly to Pusan, Korea.

That morning on the dock at Yokohama Bay, Japan was as close as I ever got to GHQ.

Years later when I retired, my military records were incomplete so I asked for (and got) a corrected record check. The Department of Defense informed me by mail that they could give me a complete record check with the exception of one part of my records: they had no record of how I got into Korea. They knew I was there, for the Department of Defense issued me five Bronze Battle Stars for the Korean Campaigns I fought in. Also orders showed me transferred three different times from one department to another. For the convenience of the military, they also knew when I left Korea. But they were unable to determine how I got to Korea in the first place.

Anyhow, you readers now know how I got there!

When I got to Pusan, Korea, I was relieved of my men and sent to

Headquarters by jeep. There I was introduced to a Major (I can't recall his name).

He said, "Sergeant, I understand you are a qualified motor sergeant."

"Yes, sir," I said.

He continued, "We have lost the one assigned to the 287th Refrigeration Mobile unit and we are in urgent need of a replacement, so you are it. Take the rest of the day off and get squared away. Probably tomorrow, I'll have the driver take you up to the front line. There you'll meet Captain Wheeler and he'll inform you what to do and who your contact will be. The driver will tale you back to your quarters. Any questions?"

"No, sir," I said.

"Good luck," he said.

"Thank you, sir," I said.

On the way back to my quarters the driver said he would be taking me to the depot probably late tomorrow night. I asked was it very far to the front?

He said, "Not far enough. We have only 12 miles to stand on. Any further than that, Sergeant, we'll be in the ocean.

"What happened to the other Sergeant?" I asked.

"You don't want to know."

"That bad huh, can you give me an idea what to expect when I get there?" I asked already knowing what I was in for, and whatever it was, it wasn't good that's for sure.

He continued. "You'll be given 20 men with trucks. Your job will be to see that food supplies are delivered to a distribution point, so the field kitchen trucks can pick up and deliver the supplies to each kitchen in the area. It's impossible to give the troops hot meals each day, especially in times like this. Also everyone who can fire a weapon is doing so. Man, these Korean's have almost got us swimming. Something is got to give."

I didn't say a word.

He continued, "I was up in the headquarters office this morning. Some of the brass was discussing the orders that had just come down. I didn't get all of it, but what I did hear there would be no more ground given, no more retreat. Under no condition will we be pushed any further!"

"I suppose what you are saying is, its Custer's Last stand," I said.

"From what I heard this morning, I'd say you've hit the nail on the head. And, Sergeant, looks as if you are going to be right in the middle of it."

I said, "I feel kind of glad the Major has assigned me to a Quartermaster outfit. After having been in four major campaigns in Germany and earning four Bronze battle stars, I was hoping I would not be in another shootout at the old corral at high noon. At least not over here like we in the Battle of the Bulge, where I became a Prisoner of War."

"Well, Sergeant, I can assure you this place will make the old corral shootout look sick. As far as being exposed and coming under fire, man, you are much safer on the line than you'll be on the open road in a truck.

I asked, "What kind of protection do you have?"

The driver said. "Each truck has a shotgun man with the driver, to return fire when fired on. If you are in your jeep, with or without a driver, you are your own shotgun man. You'll be moving food supplies most of the time at night. The food line is so critical to troops you will be well informed of your duties."

"Sergeant, this is where you'll be hanging out until you move up tomorrow. This is a bridge company out of the Engineer Battalion. They have been moved back about a month now; seems everything had moved back to Pusan. Have you ever seen as many people in town as this?"

"I can't say I have," I said, "Douglas Georgia really wasn't so big!"

Well, Sergeant, we've finally made it back through the crowd in time for dinner," he said pulling up to the mess hall.

"Corporal, is what I'm seeing-- all those boots sticking out of the back of that weapons carrier stacked up like cordwood--what I think it is?"

"Yep. The crew goes out on the battlegrounds and picks up bodies while the medical teams take care of the wounded. They (the medic's on the battlegrounds) also mark the location of the ones they have to leave so they can be found by this crew. The crew then brings them back to the portable morgue here in Pusan. The crew has just stopped by for dinner on their way to the morgue. Man, you talk about a job the crew has, let me tell you."

"Later. Let's eat dinner, and get back to the subject afterwards," I said.

"Sounds good to me, Sergeant!"

While eating lunch, the Corporal said, "Sergeant, you look troubled but I guess you have a right to be. Having already fought one war, here you are back in another one. How did this happen?"

I told my story. "That's what I've been asking myself ever since I got to Pusan this morning. Two days ago I got to Japan with 15 men I was in charge of. We met at the docks in California for the first time. I was given a roster of the men along with tickets for all of us to board a civilian ship, with verbal orders to see they got to Japan. When we arrived at Japan we were met by a truck at the docks, taken to a building issued full combat gear, put on a boat and just arrived here this morning. Then, I was relieved of my men, and here I am! I have no idea what happened.

While en-route to Japan, I learned each man had been selected, just as I had by our company, to be sent to Japan to work for General McArthur at General Headquarters (GHQ). Each one left our company in the States, thinking we were on our own. But when we met at the docks, the whole picture changed. We were no longer alone but with a group selected for a certain job in GHQ, or so we thought. Instead, here I am right back within a perimeter of 12 miles of a war. Enemy on one side and the ocean on the other. I've got to break out just like in Germany and I didn't make it out of Germany until I became a prisoner of war."

I paused, then added, "I had no idea what this job was when I was sent to Japan. But this I do know, I am well aware of what's before me and what must be done. Like it or not, it's my job."

"Well, Sergeant if you've finished your lunch, I'll take you over to your quarters, so you can meet the 1st Sergeant. He will help you get settled in as long as you are here," said the driver.

When we arrived at the Bridge Company Headquarters, the 1st Sergeant was standing in the door of his office.

As the Corporal and I approached him, he stuck out his hand.

"I am," he said, "First Sergeant Parker here, and you are Sergeant Lankford. I understand you are going to be with us a day or so on your way to the front to become the Motor Sergeant for the 287th. Refrigeration company. Sergeant how long have you been in Korea?

"This is my first day," I said.

"Oh, boy," he replied.

The strain of war was obvious on his face. I later learned he had lost quite a few of his men just a couple of week prior.

"I understand they lost their Motor Sergeant little over a week ago, and they sure need one," he said.

I said, "I will give them the best I've got."

He said, "I'm sure you will."

"Do you know what happened to the last motor Sergeant?" I asked.

He said, "You don't need to know what happened to him. All you need to know is how to do you job and keep alive. Have you been in combat?"

"Yes, plenty. I was with the 106th infantry division in Germany," I said.

"Then you were in the Battle of the Bulge?" he asked.

"Very much so."

"I understand two regiments were surrounded and delayed the German Army from advancing," he said.

"Those two regiments were the 422nd and the 423rd of the 106th Infantry Division. Also there were two Field Artillery Battalions, the 589th and the 590th. We were surrounded along with the two Regiments. I was in Company B. of the 423rd Regiment."

"I heard it was some kind of rough fighting," he said.

"Well Sergeant; you don't know the half of it," I said.

"I have an extra bed in my room if you care to stay with me," he said.

"I would like that very much too," I said.

"Come with me and I'll show you where you can put your equipment, and where your bed is," he said.

The Sergeant and I got to know a few things about each other. He was out of Alabama. We exchanged war stories well into the night. After learning how many men he had lost, it was no wonder the strain of war was showing on his face. We didn't get very much sleep that night. The Sergeant was very upset about the loss of his men. To be honest with you, I wasn't feeling too good about the situation myself. Being in a 12 mile perimeter with the enemy on one side and the ocean on the other and knowing we had to break through, was sure not looking good.

When morning came, he and I went to breakfast. Afterwards, he went about his duties. I returned to the room.

As I sat looking out of the window at all the people who had moved back from the war zone into Pusan... at all the military, which had been pushed back (The town was full of people, old and young) I noticed a lady cooking something over an open fire in a pot. It looked like some type of mush. I also saw a young boy who appeared to be somewhere around nine or ten years old. His pants was wet from the belt line down and torn. Also he wore a short sleeve shirt, dirty and torn.

He was just walking around from one family to another. He came to the lady I was looking at. She had three small children sitting on a blanket. She dipped three small bowls of the food from the pot and gave each child a bowl. When she turned to do something else, the boy took one of the children's bowls and ran off with it. He was not the only one taking food from the children. Several others were doing the same thing.

Being an ex-POW, I under stood how they felt. I know it's wrong to take something that does not belong to you, but my friend, when you are hungry all you can think is survival. I remembered my days as a POW and what it was like trying to survive on one loaf of bread with eleven other men. One days ration for the twelve of us.

As I looked at those people trying to survive with not even a place to call home, only boxes, lean-to's, and blankets stretched between too points for shelter, I was reminded of how Americans lived and how God has blessed us so richly. I thought how that same scene could very well be in America.

And to be honest with you I was a bit ashamed of myself, asking why was I over there in Korea? I knew I was there because I was a soldier. It was my job to help make sure the scene I was looking at would never happen in American. What ever the cost was.

As always in troubled times, I talked with the Lord. Not only what I was facing, but I prayed for every one of us over there. After praying, the 12 miles we were on didn't seem so small after all.

Orders had been issued. There would be no more retreating.

We did what had to be done.

I went to the 1st Sergeant and advised him I was going out into town to look around and would be back with a couple of hours.

"Wait," He said. "In a few minutes my clerk will be back and I'll go with you, I've wanted to do this for a while."

The clerk returned about half hour later. On arrival, the clerk handed the 1st Sergeant the mail. The 1st Sergeant said, "Well this message said for me to provide you with transportation up to the front at my convenience. Just so happens, I don't have a thing available until tomorrow."

Looking at the clerk, he said, "I'll check in with you all along, I'm going out for a little while. Make sure you are here when I check with you."

He looked at me and said, "Sergeant Lankford lets go."

I said, "Sergeant, "I must tell you up front, I don't drink. I have no reason to go to a bar and I won't go to one."

The Sergeant turned around and shook my hand, "That makes two of us."

We spent the day walking, looking and relaxing. We made it back to camp in time for supper. Next morning, transportation was provided to take me up to the front. While the jeep driver was helping me get my equipment into the jeep the First Sergeant came out of his office.

He said. "Well, guess you're leaving us, huh?"

"Sure looks that way," I said.

He said, "Sergeant, I just wanted to tell you again. What you and I did yesterday, getting out away from the usual, relaxing, was the best dose of medicine I've had in a long time. I think I will do it more often if I can find the time."

I said, "Sergeant, it was a good day you should do it more often. It sure helps to get out, walk and think. Forgetting about the killing a little while makes a difference. Guess here is where we say our goodbyes. Look's like the driver is ready to go."

The Sergeant looked at me a few moments, without saying any thing. Then His hand came out and so did mine. We shook and held hands a long moment.

He looked into my eyes and said, "Sergeant Lankford, be careful and take care. May God be with you." Then he turned and walked slowly away.

I said, "Same to you First Sergeant." He never looked back, just threw up his hand and kept walking. I never heard anymore from, or about Sergeant Shumaker. But I have a feeling he made it back to his family okay.

I mounted the jeep and we begin working our way through the mass of people in Town.

I asked, "How long do you think it will take us to get to the supply point?"

"I have no idea," the driver said. "But Sergeant, with all the people, military and equipment, it's going to take a while. The last time I was sent up there, about a mile from the supply point," he paused. "Sergeant, "let me ask you something?"

"Ok, I said, let it go."

"Have you ever had the front end of a jeep blown out from under you by a rocket?"

"No; and I sure hope I don't ever," I said.

He went on, "Last week about a mile from the supply point, that's what happened to me. Man, you talk about seeing stars. Stars were all I could see for a few minutes. When the rocket hit the jeep, the jeep left the road and turned over, stopping when it hit a bank. But seems I must have traveled at least 15 or more feet in the air before I ever landed. Nothing was broken, but I was all bruised up."

"I was wondering why you were walking with a limp," I said.

"I tell you this. If you don't get a jeep or truck knocked out from under you, with the job you've got, you can count yourself blessings. You'll soon find out, the enemy will do most anything to get to our food supply. Man, they'd rather go for the food than the ammunition supply. And what makes it so bad, you can't go the same route each time. Once the enemy learns your route, you have trouble getting through. Right now, we're just holding our own. I don't know what it will be like when we break out of this 12-mile limit we have. No one knows yet, but I'm thinking it's not good."

I said, "You're right corporal, it's not going to be easy. I know. I've been there before."

We drove on and finally, the driver said, "Well, Sergeant, here we are. This is where you'll be hanging out for Lord knows how long."

I was met by a Sergeant who asked me to follow him. He took me to the officer in charge to be instructed of my duties. The officer was seated at a field desk in a tent. He stopped what he was doing, looked up at me and said, "I'm sure glad to see you Sergeant."

"Thank you, sir," I said. "Wish I could say the same, but I'm not too happy being here."

"I know how you feel, and you're not alone. It sure looks like things are going to get a lot worse. Right now, we're just holding our own. Shortly we will be breaking out of the perimeter and start-kicking butt. If you will go with the Corporal, he'll show you where to store your equipment and bunk down while we are here."

In a day or so, more surprises! We were on the move, and I was not a motor sergeant!

Someone found out I had combat experience. Yep, you guessed it! Next thing I knew I was leading a squad of men into battle and memories of the battles I had been through in Germany jumped on me like a wild cat. I could not shake them.

To be honest with you, I cannot remember how the battles in Korea went. They seemed like a dream and I still cannot put them in perspective. I must have done something right for I was awarded five Bronze Battle Stars for Korea. I don't know — in detail — how I got them, and again, I don't ever want to know.

One thing I do know, it wasn't good. I just thank God for letting me do what was expected of me and bringing me back home again. But I don't want to leave you with a complete blank as to how the battles in Korea went.

I started writing this book and wasn't able to remember in detail just how the battles went. So I did some research on the Korea War Battles. I can only share with you what I learned from my research.

The story of the famed 27th Infantry Regiment in Korea that I came up with in my research is a personal story.

This was taken from: *The Korean War Project*.

I was there and fought with them. At times, in war, you don't know who, or what unit you are fighting with. Anyway, on the research indication, points to the Author as Sergeant First Class. (Ret.) George Langdale. From the few memories I recall, I find his story to be true.

At the end of WWII, Korea was divided at the 38th parallel into communist North and the democratic South. The Soviets actively organized the North Korean Army (NKA) with the intent of invading South Korea. On the 25th of June 1950, the NKA crossed the 38th parallel and invaded South Korea, President Truman, in conjunction with the United Nations (UN) condemned the invasion and deployed US forces to Korea to repel the aggression. There were no US combat units in South Korea at that time. The closest units were in Japan on occupation duty.

When the war broke out, the regiment was in Japan training. The Wolfhounds were soon chosen to lead the 25th infantry Division deployment to Korea. In command of the regiment was Lieutenant Colonel ("Mike") Michaelis (pronounced Ma-KAY-less), and he lead the Wolfhounds to great fame during his command. In Korea he would receive two battlefield promotions within six months, to full Colonel and Brigadier General. General Michaelis was an exemplary and hard leader who believed in intense and demanding training. Before moving to its area of operation, he assembled his officers and non-commission officers and told them he wanted the men stripped down to weapons, a canteen of water, and rations, All else would be discarded. Colonel Michaels had studied oriental fighting tactics and jungle warfare during WWII. He told his leaders to always take the high ground looking over their position, have the men to drink a full canteen of water in the morning, then refill the canteen and ensure a proper level of body fluids throughout the day.

Concluding the talk, Colonel Michaels said, "Remember, you're here to kill and not to be killed."

The regiment landed by ship at Pusan, Korea on 10 July 1950 and was immediately thrust into battle to stem the rushing NKA. The regiment moved to Uisong, approximately 35 miles north of Taegu. They received orders on the 13 July to move to Sangju but enroute they were diverted to Hawanggan. From 24 to 29 July, The regiment fought the NKA's 2nd Division at Hawanggan. On 24 July, during engagement at Hawanggan, the 1st Battalion clandestinely disengaged while covering the regiment's withdrawal. As dawn broke the next morning, the NKA, thinking the Wolfhounds were exposed, attacked into the vacated position. They were greeted by the combined fire of tanks, artillery, mortar, and small arms into the massive engagement area. The two NKA Battalions were destroyed. During operations around Hawanggan, the regiment inflected over 3,000 casualties, before withdrawing on order, at a cost of 53 KIA, (Killed in action) 221, WIA, (Wounded in action) and a MIA, (Missing in action). Other US and South Korean (ROK) units were retreating in disorder. This was the first action in which a US unit skillfully fought the NKA to a standstill and still remained combat ready. For this action, the regiment was awarded the Presidential Unit Citation of the war.

Retreating US and ROK forces consolidated and moved into defensive operations around the port city of Pusan in southeast Korea. The Regiment moved into the US Eight Army's reserve. The Wolfhounds quickly become known as the 8th Army's "Fire Brigade," rushing to destroy NKA units who had broke through the defense.

The next Wolfhound fight would earn the regiment's second Presidential Unit Citation. The NKA surrounded ROK Units near

Pohang and continue moving towards Taegu, in the northern sector of the Pusan Perimeter. Wolfhounds and 23rd Regiment dug in along Tabu Road leading to Taegu and prepared to defend. The NKA 13 Division, leading the attack, collided with the Wolfhounds the 18th August. The Wolfhounds were fully prepared for a hard fight, mines laid, flares ready, all guns zeroed in.

When the enemy came into range, Michaelis turned loose a hail of frightening and deadly fires. Two NKA tanks, an artillery piece, two trucks and over 100 enemy troops were destroyed. The same scene was repeated for seven consecutive nights. The Wolfhounds Battalion commander remained magnificently cool and refused to yield one yard of ground. Bit by bit they whittled down the strength of the enemy division inflicting 4000 casualties. The persistent and noisy onrush of the NKA down this alley, coupled with tank and return firing, reminded the Wolfhounds of a bowling alley. This resolute stand was of course named the *Battle of the Bowling Alley.*

The Eighth Army Commander, General Walton Walker, inspected the Wolfhound front on 20 August, Surveying the NKA carnage on the battlefield and the stout American positions. He declared, "Taegu is certainly saved." On 31 August the NKA defeated, the Regiment went into reserve near Masan.

On 15 September 1950, General Douglas MacArthur conducted the amphibious assault at Inchon which would eventually cut off the NKA at the Pusan perimeter. On 19 September US units attacked out of the perimeter. The Wolfhounds, attacking westward against retreating NKA units captured Chin-ju on 28 September, secured the Chig-ni and Chonju Road and began mop-up operations. The landing at Inchon and the break out of the Pusan perimeter decisively broke the NKA's back and precipitated their withdrawal from South Korea.

The Korean War took a decisive turn when President Truman decided to invade North Korea and re-unite the two countries. From October through November 1950, UN forces pursued the NKA across the 38th parallel towards the Yale River`, which divided North Korea from Red China. In early October through November, 27th Regiment was involved in the clearing the Triangle near Chorwon. The retreating NKA used the Triangle as a guerrilla base operations, and ambushes. On 6 November the Regiment's I and R platoon (Scouts) and a platoon from L company were ambushed near Kunch-On and Sibyon-ni. Fourteen Americans were murdered when they refused to give their captors information other than rank, and serial number.

On 25 November 1950, the Regiment stopped for Thanksgiving Dinner near the Kuryang River and a small North Korean Village named Ipsok. MacAuthur announced the Korean "Police

Action" was almost over and the troops would be home for Christmas. The 25th Division part of the US I Corp launched an advance towards Unson. The Regiment was designated as the Corps reserve. However, Chinese Communist Forces (CCF) had another plan. They moved six armies over the border into North Korea. They savagely attacked UN forces on 25 November, causing a retreat across the entire front.

Captain Reginald Desiderio gave his life protecting the task force command post. He was wounded numerous times, but still managed to encourage his men. He moved up and down the line shouting, "Hold on'til daylight! Hold on'til daylight, and we've got it made!" He received the medal of Honor posthumously for his action.

Forced to conduct a fighting withdrawal, the 25th Division and the Wolfhounds withdrew to Yongbyon and then Sukchon, taking up defensive positions. Further retreats were ordered to the Imjin River and finally to Pyongtaek in early January, the Division took up positions along line D. The CCF offensive had pushed US and UN out of North Korea and northern, South Korea and recaptured Seoul. The capital during retreat, the Wolfhounds were frequently called upon to cover the withdrawal. Of other U.S. units always fighting hard and in good order.

Since only the Chinese offensive UN forces had retreated, morale was low, almost no offensive spirit remain. General Ridgeway, who took command of the 8th Army in early December, desperately needed to restore the Americans fighting spirit. Calling upon Michaelis's Wolfhounds, he ordered the Regiment to attack in early January 1951. Although Wolfhounds encountered no resistance, its aggressive deployment forward of "line D. Served as an important moral builder. The Eighth Army was no longer withdrawing, but attacking.

In mid January, another attack was launched, code name "Wolfhound" attacking north, the Regiment cleared Osan advanced to Wason, withdrawing only when in danger of being trapped. This attack, like the early one provided the allied forces another much needed psychological uplift.

From late January to mid February, the fighting in Korea was characterized by attacks and counter attacks, Colonel (the Captain) "Lewis Millett, earned the medal of Honor when he led Easy Company, 2nd Battalion and 27th Infantry in a bayonet assault on a fortified Chinese hilltop. It was described by Army historian as "…the greatest bayonet attack by US soldiers since Cold Harbor in the Civil War". Colonel Michaelis was promoted to Brigadier General and the 27th

Regiment command was passed on to Colonel Gilbert Check, who had command the 1st Battalion since the beginning of the war. On 16th February 1951, the Wolfhounds, as part of the 25th Infantry Division, attacked north to the Han River under a massive artillery barrage. Eleven artillery batteries alone supported the Regiment. This assault in conjunction with other attacks early January, forced the CCF and the NKA forces to withdraw from South Korea.

March 7, 1951 preceded by tremendous artillery preparation, the Regiment spearheaded by the third Battalion led an assault across the Han River near Mugam, this 25th Division advanced, outflanked the communist forces in Seoul and shortly caused the enemy to withdraw from the South Korean Capital. The Regiment continued its advance from the Han River until it was relieved near Uijonbu. On 3 April, the 27th was again on the attack as part of Operation "Rugged," crossed the 38th parallel, where the war had begun months earlier. The Regiment received its third Presidential Unit citation for actions during the crossing of the Han River.

From early mid April, The Regiment continued its advance north finally reaching Line Utah, near Chorwon. On 22 April advanced further to Line Wyoming. That same night the CCF attacked again, its objective the recapture of Seoul. Hantan River, six Chinese Divisions with 50,000 troops struck again the 27th and the 24th Infantry Regiments, The CCF hit the left sector of the Wolfhounds hard with artillery, infantry, and several tanks. In another remarkable performance the Regiments held in close, hand to hand fighting. The CCF then backed off in the dark, then hit the right sector of the Wolfhounds.

A senior Officer remembered, "It was a machine gunner's and artilleryman's dream. The Reds came swarming across the rice paddies in mass formation. Eighth Artillery batters, all the machine guns available, and several tanks poured in rapid fire. After about thirty minutes, the Reds had enough. The remnants retreated, carrying all the wounded they could and leaving a thousand dead and wounded behind.

The Wolfhounds were not bothered anymore that day.

By the 24th April, the CCF offensive was at full fury and caused the withdrawal of the Division to the Line Lincoln, where they prepared defensive positions, north of the Han River and Seoul. The Wolfhounds mission was to defeat and inflict maximum casualties. From 28 to the 30 April, the CCF attacked. But due to overwhelming artillery, and the combat proficiency of the US forces, This Line Lincoln remained unbroken. CCF withdrew to Uijonbu to lick his wounds. This Chinese attack, known as the spring Offensive, was the single biggest battle of the war.

From the end of April through mid May 1951, the 27th Regiment continued to hold Line Lincoln, northeast of Seoul, awaiting another communist offensive. However, the Chinese renewed their attack further east, in an attempt to envelope the Eighth Army and Seoul from the southeast. To counter this offensive UN forces in the east withdrew, then counterattacked in the west, 1 Corps (of which the 25th division and the Regiment were assigned) also attacked north to Line Kansas at the Han River on 20 May, achieving its objective on 28 May.

Next the Wolfhound participated in Operation Pile driver, which again placed it near the Iron Triangle, at Kumhwa. Pile driver began in June 1951, and Kumhaw was secured on 14 June, the Wolfhounds dug in, built bunkers, strung wire, planted mines, and registered its artillery. The lull in battle ended on 12 September when the Regiment attacked and seized heavily fortified communist fortification near Kumhwa. Lieutenant Sudut, a platoon leader with B Company, was awarded the Medal of Honor after he lost his life single-handedly by storming an enemy bunker which had pinned down his platoon. Over fifty other Wolfhounds received medals for valor actions during the attack. Shortly afterward, the 25th Division, to include the Wolfhounds, was relieved on Line Kansas and became the 1 Corps reserve.

One story stands out in my mind. After a nasty battle one day, a runner from Headquarters in Pusan came up to the line. When he found me, he said the Battalion Commander wanted to see me; to bring me back.

"Did you check with my Captain?" I said.

"Yes!" He told me where to find you. So grab what you have and lets go," he said.

"Grab what I have? My friend you're looking at it!"

"Man! When was the last time you washed, shaved, and changed clothes?"

"What's That? Something new came out" I said" Troop, we haven't had time to do anything around here but fight.

"Well, when we leave here we will go by supply where you can clean up and get a changing of clothes. You sure can't go to the Commander's office looking like this, he said.

" Why not? I sure haven't been sitting behind a desk with my feet propped up drinking coffee lately."

"Look, Sergeant, its fine with me, if you want to go to the Commander's office like you are.

I will surely take you if you want. I just thought you would like to shower, shave, and clean up. Put on some clean clothes. It would make you feel better," he said.

"I guess you're right, Corporal. I just wasn't thinking," I said.

"It's okay, Sergeant. In a place like this we don't have time to think, just respond."

"You're right again, Corporal, so lets go."

As we traveled he said, "Sergeant, while I was at Headquarters waiting for a run—messengers sit around waiting to be sent out—so, three days ago. I heard the Commander talking with the Lieutenant in charge of the messengers. The Commander wanted some man found and brought back off of the front, Now! The Commander sounded upset. The Lieutenant closed the door to the office. After a few minutes, the Lieutenant came out of the office, looked at me and said, let's go! We went outside to the jeep. The Lieutenant told me to find Sergeant J.D. Lankford. He's somewhere on the line fighting, and not to come back with out you."

I said, "Must be important?"

He said, "The Lieutenant, told me what the Colonel had said. This man had seen enough fighting. He was in the Battle of the Bulge, and a Prisoner of War in Germany tipping the scales at 93 pounds when liberated, I know there's something for him to do besides fighting. I've spent most of the last three days looking for you. I don't think you will be up here again fighting, unless things get out of hand. And the way thing are looking, I don't look for that to happen."

"I sure hope you are right. I've had all of the fighting I care to be involved in. What ever he's got for me will be welcome without hesitation!" I said.

When we got to the clothes supply building, the supply Sergeant looked at me and said,

"You look awful, man."

"I feel awful," I said.

"How about a good shower?"

"Just point me in the right direction," I said.

"Go in that door turn right first door on right."

"Thanks," I said.

He called, "I'll bring you some clothes, what size?

"32-31-pants, 15-32 shirt, shorts-undershirts medium. 8½ boots."

"Gotcha. You will find shaving equipment in the cabinet, if you would like to shave."

"Thank you, I said again.

After the shave, shower, and getting dressed, we were on our way to Headquarters. I reported to the colonel. He said." "Don't tell me you have just come out of combat looking like that?"

"No Sir, I didn't. The driver sidetracked me over to the clothes supply for a shave, shower, and some clean clothes," I said.

"It's like hell up there isn't it? He asked,

"It's sure not heaven, sir," I said.

"I know, Sergeant. I had you brought back when I learned you were in War over in Germany. The battles you were in and how you became a prisoner of war. When General Patton got you out of the POW Camp, and over to the hospital in France, your medical records show you're weight was 93 pounds, is that right?"

"Yes, sir." I said.

"I understand you went up as a motor Sergeant?" He asked.

"Yes, sir."

"Didn't last long, did it?" he said.

"No, sir, it didn't. I was told I was needed more as a squad leader because I had combat experience and was a seasoned Infantryman," I said. "In fact, my job as Motor Sergeant ended right after the breakout, and things got hot and nasty."

"Sergeant, I have a major, a veterinarian, and he wants to be relieved of his extra duty running the cold storage and Ice Plant here in Pusan. I think you are just the one we are looking for. He has 22 men with trucks assigned to the plant. Their jobs are to drive trucks bringing in frozen food supplies from the ships unloading at the docks, to the cold storage and then it is shipped out to the troops. A shipment goes out every day at 5:30 in the evening by train. You will be given a

shipping order for frozen items each day, which is to be on the train on
or before 5:30 each evening. That's a must. In case you're wondering
about labor, there's an office stocked with well trained personnel and
an interpreter. Laborers to unload the trucks and stack the supplies in
storage are furnished each day from the labor pool. Labor details come
in groups of ten men plus the leader of the group."

I said, "Got it."

He continued, "Two groups are assigned each day as regulars.
They come every day, they know what must be done, and how to do it.
Now, that's one Must. Here is another one. The US military has control
of the Ice plant as well as the cold storage. Both are operations are
located in the same building. The building is located on another dock
on the other side of town. Its docking is not deep enough for large ships
to dock there, that's why we have to truck the frozen food from the ship
to the cold storage. The fishing boats have to come there for crushed
Ice they need for fishing.

The owners operate the ice plant. All maintenance on compressors
and electrical problems with both the plant and cold storage are under
the control of our military. Once a week they will submit a list of
supplies they need to keep the old equipment operating. We furnish all
the supplies needed. When you get the list of supplies requested,
always, before ordering check the list carefully. They will try getting
anything they can to get you too fill the request for them. If you think
any part of the request is not needed, strike it off of the list. Sometimes
you will have to physically check the equipment to make sure the parts
are needed. Sergeant, do you think you'll make the Major happy and
take it off of his hands?" he asked.

"Colonel, sir, I'll tackle anything," I said.

The Colonel said, "That I believe. The driver will take you over to
the plant. The Major will clue you in on the details. If you have any
problem you can't handle, come see me. And good luck Sergeant."

"Thank you, sir," I said.

On the way to the freezer plant, the driver said, "Sergeant, I don't know
what to tell you about the major at the plant. One thing I do know, he
sure don't like being tied down with the plant."

He doesn't, huh?"

"Lord no so don't let him get next to you." he said.

"Oh he won't. He probably will be so glad to be leaving, he won't
even think about being mean.

When we got to the plant, the driver directed me to the office.

The Major met us at the door, with a big smile on. He asked, " You're Sergeant Lankford?"

"Yes, sir," I had no name tag on.

"Man, I sure am glad to see you. The Colonel called and said you were on you're way. I've been doing two jobs for weeks now running this place and trying to be a doctor."

"Who was here before you? I asked.

"He was a Lieutenant needed else where. We've lost a lot of Lieutenants since the breakout, and most everyone has doubled up on their jobs."

"Sir, I don't know how it has been back here. But it sure is not a picnic up front," I said.

I know, Sergeant. War is pure hell."

"You're right about that, Sir," I agreed.

He said, "When the Colonel called, letting me no you were on your way, I knew you would need to know something about what's going on. So I prepared a list of the main things you will have to know. Look over it, and if you can think of anything else you may need I'll be glad to help any way I can.

"This Man, Tony," he said, pointing towards a young man who had just walked in is your interpreter, He has been with us since we came to the plant. He was an English teacher in the school system here in Pusan and you'll do well to rely on him. I sure had to. He knows how the Cold Storage and the Ice Plant Operates."

I shook hands with Tony.

"The doctor added, "I have left my phone number and how to get in touch with me on your desk. If you're not sure about something, give me a call. If I can't help you, I'll get someone who can. I'll have them to get in touch with you. Do you have any questions?"

"Not that I can think of," I said.

"Good luck, Sergeant."

"Thank you, sir," the Major turned, smiled as he walked away."

"Well, Tony, looks like you and I have a plant to run."

"Yes, sir, we sure do. But we can do it," said Tony.

"Yep, that we can. And first on the agenda, let's get acquainted with the office personnel," I said.

The door on the back of my new office opened into a large work room. As I entered, I counted fifteen desks a clerk working at each desk. There was an odd, empty desk. I asked Tony about it.

"Oh," he said. "That's the office supervisor's desk. Pointing to a lady walking around the office, checking each persons work. She was one of my students in school. She reads and speaks very good English. You will find her very efficient in her job." Tony motioned for her to come over to where we were, and introduced her. He said, "Every one calls her Moon."

How long have you been here, Moon?" I asked.

"Ever since the Army has had the plant, sir," she said.

Do you like your job?"

"Yes, sir, very much," she said.

"Good, how many of your work force speaks English?"

"Out of the five men, only three; the girls, only four," she said.

"At a more convenient time I'd like to speak with each one of them. Tony, will let you know when," I said.

Tony asked, "Would you like to meet the Ice plant personnel?"

"I can't think of a better time than now. Can you?"

"No, sir," he said.

We entered the Ice plant and met the President and his three Vice Presidents. I supposed the expression on my face must have caught Tony's attention when the President introduced three Vice Presidents! Tony immediately explained that the three Vice Presidents were assigned to the three main departments of the operation of the ice and cold storage plants: Electrical, Refrigeration and Maintenance. And each department had nine men assigned to them, working three, eight hour shifts with three men each. The only one who could speak English was one man, the chief refrigeration foreman.

I didn't get to meet the truck drivers until after 5:30 o'clock in the evening because they were busy moving frozen supplies to the cold storage until after seven o'clock in the evening. But after about an hour with the men, my opinion was they were dedicated to their job and seemed to be Soldiers not just hired labors. Their only complaint was they were missing so many meals. They had no problem with breakfast, but the dinner and supper meals were scarce. They said maybe they'd get a hot meal three or four times a week but the rest of the time it was sandwiches or nothing.

After a week or so, I got my feet on the ground by getting involved in every phase of the operation. The military drivers did a magnificent job. Office personnel, likewise. Everything worked as it should, making my job easy. About a month on the job, a captain—the commanding officer of Engineer Company—had asked if he could talk with me a few minutes. I asked him to join me in the office. After we were seated, the Captain leaned forward and said, "Sergeant Lankford, I've been wanting to come."

"I'm glad you did sir, what's on your mind?" (I knew he must want something, I had already been through that routine with some Nurses from the Swedish Hospital here in Pusan).

"I want to give my company a little party. My First Sergeant is having a Birthday in a couple of days. I'm sure you're aware there is no accountability on supplies in a combat zone."

"Yes, sir, I know that," I said.

"Sergeant, I was hoping you could help me out with a few item for the party."

I said, "Captain, you're just the person I've been looking for. I'll give you all you need, and maybe you can help me. I have a problem with my military personal getting their meals due to their work schedule. They have no problem with breakfast. It's lunch and supper. They won't average getting a hot lunch or supper over three or four times a week. It's bag meals or nothing the rest of the time. In order for me to take care of this problem, I need a few things myself."

"Tell me what you need," he said.

"I need a field stove with cooking utilities. I have a large storage room on the second floor, that would make a fine kitchen and a lunch room. Also I need lumber to build tables and benches for about thirty people. Someway or another, I'm going to see my men get three hot meals a day."

"Sergeant, I have a sergeant in my company. I don't know how, when, or where, and I don't ask. But I only have to say I need something, and very shortly it shows up as company property. When do you want the order delivered?"

Within a week I had a full stocked Kitchen up and going.

About three months later, a Captain came into my office. He informed me he was from Regimental Headquarters and would like to have a few moments of my time, if he could, (when an officer asks a Sergeant if they can have a few moments of their time, brother, you can expect anything to happen).

I said, "Would you care to sit down, Captain?"

He obliged. Then he leaned forward and said; "Sergeant, what do you think about receiving a field commission as a 2nd lieutenant?"

"I hadn't thought anything about it, sir," I said.

"You know the job you are doing calls for an officer," he said.

"I figured it did; I relieved a major when I came here. The major said that he was doing two jobs since he relieved the Lieutenant that was here for front line duty. He was trying to be a Dr. (veterinarian) and run this plant. I wondered then how long it would be before I had a boss here with me."

"Sergeant, the problem is, there are no lieutenants to put here. We have lost so many lieutenants in combat; we just don't have a lieutenant to put here."

"Captain, how long do you think I would be here doing this job as an officer, before I would be back in battle. Not as a squad leader with nine men, but as a platoon leader with 36 men plus?" I said.

"The way things are going right now, maybe two weeks. And you can safely bet on that. I was sent by the Regimental Commander to see how you felt about it," he said.

"Truthfully, I don't think much about it. I've had all of the fighting I care to have," I said `

"The Commander said you probably would say something like that. And he would understand. He doesn't want you to have to go back up there. I came up with an idea you might want to think about. I have a one way ticket home for you if you care to go for it?"

"Captain, if it is a way out of this place and home, let's hear about it," I said.

"If you were to apply for Officers Candidate School and nothing in regulations states you cannot go to school if you qualify. There's no question about you not being qualified to go to school. All you have to do is apply for it. I'll handle the rest of it for you," he said.

I didn't know what to think.

"Now, you need to understand this. After graduation it don't mean you won't be sent back over here. That could very well happen if this mess keep's going like it is. If you don't want to come back here after graduation as an officer, you have two choices. One is fail the OCS school. But you don't want to do that. It is well known you are qualified to complete the school and to fail would not look good at all. Second choice is resign just prior to graduation. You will have to give an excuse as to why and the best I know is just say you decided you don't want to be an officer. You can expect them to ask you why and

I'm sure you can come up with something."

I said "Where do I get an application?"

"I'll get you one just give me a few days. When I get it, I'll help you fill it out, and get it approved for you."

"Thanks, Captain," I said.

"Oh," he said. "There's one more thing we have to count on to get the application approved. I will have to explain why you want to go to school to get a commission when one was offered you here. And it better be good."

"Captain, it's like the old farmer always said, don't change a horse in the middle of a stream, unless the horse has been trained for the job required of him. I don't know how to be an officer with out being trained to do so. One thing I do know, an officer has a greater responsibility, especially in combat. The decision he makes determines if a mother's son goes home to the family he loves or to his own funeral. Making decisions on choices or lucky calls don't work, where life or death decisions must be made. If I was commissioned now, even if it was weeks from now, and I was called to lead a platoon of men into combat, I would still be a Sergeant in an officer's uniform. That won't work. I know a Sergeant's job. I don't an Officer's. If I'm going to be an officer, then train me. Or, just let me be a Sergeant. I know how to do that. As far as becoming an officer, I won't be sure until prior to graduation, if I'm allowed to go to OCS school."

"Sergeant, give me a few days to look into this and I will get back to you," he said.

"Thank you, sir," I said.

I didn't hear from the captain for a little over three weeks. Then one day he walked into my office with a big smile on.

He said, "Pack your bags. I got your request for OCS approved. You should be on your way home within a week."

The captain was right. Four days later I was on my way to Japan for shipment back to the states, with a 15 day delay in route to go home before reporting for school. I left Korea and arrived in Japan around 10:30 in the morning. By 3:30 in the afternoon, I was processed, received my orders, and hitched a ride on a military plane for California I arrived in California and had about two hours layover. But before I could catch another military plane for Jacksonville, Florida, I called my wife, letting her know I would be coming into Cecil Field Military Air Base, at Jacksonville. The pilot said he would not get there until around

8:30 in the morning.

"I'll be there waiting for you." she said, "and, oh! Those were words I had been waiting to hear for so long.

We arrived at Cecil Field on time. My wife and boys were there. We were on our way home very shortly. It was only 75 miles home, so we arrived around noon to a big country meal at my mother-in-law's house.

After the leave of 15 days, I reported to OCS school at Fort Riley, Kansas. The class in progress was a week away from graduation. Before a new class begin. The school Commandant gave me time to get my family moved from Georgia to Kansas. We got moved, settled in and still had a day left before a new class started. I liked the school very much in fact I liked what I was taught in school. I had to wrestle with myself about graduating. Should or should I not? Four days before graduating. The Should not won out. The Commandant wasn't happy at all accepting my letter of resignation. The Captain back in Korea was correct. When he said the Commandant would want to know why I resigned from school, I gave him the reason I had given the Captain back in Korea.

"Sergeant, I can understand how you must feel, and if there was a way I could assure you would not have to go back to Korea and have any more combat duty I would. I'm sure you understand I can't. Graduating is the chance you'll have to take. I'm sure you realize your schooling is over. There's only four days left. We'll spend three days reviewing what the class had learned. The last day is graduation. In reality, you have completed the school. If you won't accept the commission, I understand, and will accept your resignation."

Thank you, sir," I said and started to leave. I got almost to the door.

He called, "Sergeant."

I stopped did about face and said, "Sir?"

He looked at me for a moment and said, "Sergeant, I'm really sorry."

"Thank you, sir," I saluted then did about face and left the room.

I was transferred to a quartermaster section at Fort Riley Kansas. I was assigned duty with the post commissary officer, Major Prudhone operating the commissary. I was put in charge of ordering perishable food supplies for the commissary and troop consumption for the base.

In 1952, a couple of months prior to reenlistment for another three years of service, Mildred asked me if I would consider asking for another tour of duty in Germany.

"Of course I will, if you can give me a good enough reason why I should!"

"I would like to go to Germany, it would be a great experience for me and the boys. You have plenty of leave time, we can go on vacation, see the country and for sure I want to take the boys to the POW camp where you were. If you think it would not bother you."

I said, "Mill, I have no problem with going back to Germany, what so ever. I think it would be good, not only for you and the boys, but for all of us. But first there's something you will have to understand. If I, as an ex-POW in the military, return to Germany where I was held as a prisoner of war, I will have to be cleared by the Department of Defense. I'll have to sign a waver that I hold no malice against the German people for what happened."

"J.D.," she said, "look me straight in the eyes and tell me: do you have any malice against the German people?"

"No, of course not." I said.

"Then we don't have a problem do we?"

I said, "Not on my part, we don't," I said.

"What do you say we go for it?" she said.

"Girl, you're on."

I got a waiver approved before re-enlistment. Things went very good after re-enlistment. I was assigned to the 22nd Quartermaster Subsistence Supply Company in Manheim, Germany.

When I arrived at my company in Germany, I was placed on TDY (Temporary Duty) to a coffee roasting plant in Neunburg, Germany, as NCOIC (Non-Commission Officer In Charge) of operating the plant.

It was almost three months before my family and car got to Germany. When the family arrived, I was relieved of my plant duty. The military had moved my family into quarters over a week before I could get replaced and return to my company in Manheim.

When the military got the house to be used as our quarters, some kind of an arrangement was made where the owner of the house (a lady) could remain living in the house on the third floor, if it was agreeable with the family assigned to the quarters. This house had nineteen rooms,

My wife accepted the house before I got there. I wasn't pleased that we would be living in the house with someone else. I was much more satisfied after learning the lady had a private entrance to her apartment.

The lady, and I say lady with all respect for she proved to be a great lady over and over, the three years we lived in the house. Her Name was Mrs. Bartle and she was a warm, loving, caring, person. Our boys fell in love with her. Mrs. Bartle's husband, who was deceased, was one of the men who designed the BMW Motor for the BMW car. All of the houses in that area were three stories. Doctors and their families lived on both sides of the Bartle, house. Lawyers lived two blocks down the street. Our garden was so large the military supplied a gardener to keep it up.

After three months, we were ready to take the trip Mildred and I had planned for, and one of the reasons we had come to Germany. Go to the POW prison camp.

We got to Bad-Orb, Germany. The former POW camp was located about four miles up the mountain. It was called Stalag 9B."

We arrived at the camp and I can't explain the feeling that came over me. And I could not shake it.

When we stopped the car and got out, Mildred knew something was wrong with me. Being the person she was, she didn't say anything just took me by the hand as we strolled through the camp, or what was left of it.

When we started home, Mildred asked if she could drive. I was sure glad she did for the feeling I got when I first got into the camp, was still with me. And we had been at camp well over two hours.

When we left for home, we cleared the gate, or where the gate had been for the prison, not more than a half mile down the roar, that feeling I had was gone. And I cannot recall ever having that unexplainable feeling again.

Six months prior to returning to the States, Mildred and I went on a 30 day-tour vacation. Our tour took us to: Holland, Belgium, France, Denmark, Spain, England, Switzerland and the Allied Zones of Germany. The most beautiful drive we made was driving through the Brenner Pass, through the Swiss Alps. After my tour of duty was over, and we returned to the States, I was assigned to a Field Artillery Missile Battalion, in Cromwell, Connecticut on arriving at the base, I found I had been assigned to the same company my brother was in. I was assigned as section Sergeant of "B" section, and I assigned my brother as section panel operator, controlling the missiles.

My brother and I worked together almost two years. When the military came out with the Hercules Missile. Which carried a nuclear warhead, I was selected to go to electronic school on the maintenance and installation of the war head into the missile.

The military moved me, family, and everything on PCS (permanent change of station) orders to Fort Bliss, Texas for my schooling. After graduation (nine months later) I was transferred on PCS orders, along with family to a Missile base, in Edgewood, Maryland as chief of electrical and maintenance on the Hercules missile.

As usual, being a soldier, I expected most anything at any given time. I had gotten settled into my new job just over a year (not sure of the exact time;) and the military opened a new site in Albany, Georgia. Albany was only about one hundred miles from my home in Broxton, Georgia. One morning, while visiting the first sergeant's office, the Commanding Officer asked me to come into his office. He informed me he had received a request for me to be transferred to the new missile base in Albany, Georgia, as Electrical and Maintenance Chief on the missile," he said, "Sergeant, you look a bit puzzled. Something wrong?"

'Sir, I was wondering why the first sergeant didn't mention it?" I asked.

"Because I told him not to. I wanted to talk with you first. And see how you felt about it."

"Captain, its not that my family and I are not happy with the assignment here. The past three years had been very good for all of us, and I've enjoyed my work, (also) if I was transferred,
you would not be left empty handed. My assistant Sergeant Walter, who I've been training him on the job now for over a year. I know, he has not been to school for the job, and I also know I was not trained one on one in school like I have trained him. And I feel sure, if push comes to shove, Sergeant Walter could and would do the job."

He said, "Sergeant, I sure hate to see you go. I also know if I had a chance to be assigned close to my home I would not turn it down. And too, you have only about three years to retirement, right?"

"More than three, sir," I said.

"There's one more catch to the move. All the key personnel in the company you are going to are leaving in about a week for schooling at Fort Bliss Texas. All the Intercept and firing control (IFC) personnel

and the Missile Launching Control (MLC) personnel, Company
Commander and the First sergeant will be in training for six months,
plus; You will have the job as First Sergeant for the rest of the
company along with 1st Lieutenant Aldridge, acting company
Commander until the rest of the company return from Fort, Bliss Texas.
We will have you on your way within a week, the holdup is the movers
hopefully that will be taken care of very shortly."

They got us moved in the Radium Springs area in Albany,
Georgia. When we arrived, I had been assigned to A. Battery, 2nd
Missile Artillery Battalion. Albany, Georgia. I remained there until I
retired in 1963.

On returning home, I opened a T.V. and radio repair shop. That
lasted 25 years. I retired from this and went into trucking. I had five 18-
wheelers on the road. "Miss" Mildred, my wife, was a beautician and
had her own shop. The Lord called her home in 1981, after an accident.

Our three children, two boys and one girl were married with their
own home and families.
I was left alone with a big house.

After more than a year living alone me knowing Miss Mildred
would not want me to live this way, I got married.

My present wife, Miss Debbie, was no stranger to our family. Miss
Mildred used to fix her hair after Miss Mildred passed away; Miss
Debbie spent a lot of time with my children and their families. Miss
Debbie also lived alone.

My children often ask her to come by my house and bring me food
and check to see if I needed anything. Usually, she visited after work
when she was on her way home. I always ask her to help me dispose of
the food she brought, my children always sent more than I needed.

One day, she said she would eat with me for she didn't feel like
going home and cooking That did it! We both enjoyed the meal and
each other company. We decided we had a good thing going, but not
pleased about someone else feeding us.

While Debbie and I were eating one evening, I offered to supply
the food if she wanted to come by and cook. That way we would not
feel guilty about someone else furnishing our meals.

"If that is what you think you would like, then I think it would be
good. When do we start?" she said.

"Tomorrow I'll let the family know what's going on. You can
check and see what supplies we need before you go home. I will have

them tomorrow when you get here."

That arrangement worked well for both us, for about a year. Miss Debbie always prepared my noon meals while cooking our evening meal, before she went home. I always made my own breakfast.

We were having our evening meal one day, when I announced I was going to take the truck and go on the road. My son Ronald could handle the trucks here at home.

She said, "I'm going with you."

"Deb!" I said, "You can't do that!"

"I'm thinking seriously about it. You're not leaving me behind!"

I said, "You know I'm a deacon in the Baptist Church. What do you think my church family would say or do?"

She said, "I'm a Sunday School teacher at the Church of God. What do you think would happen to me?"

I said, "Well, I guess there's only one way out of it. We'll have to get married. What do you say to that?"

Her reply was, "When do you want to set the date?"

"Are you sure that's what you want?" I said.

"You're not leaving me back here," she said.

So we got married in December 1982, bought another truck and went on the road. We ran most of the United states and had a wonderful time for two years until we decided to come home and run locally.

As I sit here closing out the writing of this book. I'm looking out of the window of our cabin in Georgia's Blue Ridge Mountains. The leaves have fallen, leaving the trees open so I can see the mountain sides and valleys clearly. They are beautiful and I'm enjoying the company of my gal, Miss Debbie, who has been my strength and leaning post going on twenty-seven years.

I told her I was going fishing when I turn 105 years old, and she has promised to take me.

I'm looking forward to that day.

Awards display, WWII and the Korean War and over 21 years of service.

Woodrow Mixon and J.D. Lankford the two surviving WWII P.O.W.'s in Coffee County, Georgia with Rep. Jack Kingston

Buford, W.T. Lankford, Brothers and me J.D. Lankford

W.C. Lankford, Brother

Raymond Lankford, Brother

Iris and James Daniel Lankford, Mom and Dad

W.C. and Joanne Lankford, Brother and Sister in Law

**Mildred and J.D. Lankford and children,
Ronnie, Christine and Donnie**

J.D. and Debbie Lankford

Acknowledgments

To:

My loving wife Debbie for the patience she had in listening to me as I re-lived the military part of my life again and again. The long hours that she helped me type and organize this book. Without her love and support it would not have been possible for me to write this book.

Peggy Mercer for editing this book and for encouragement and guidance so graciously given. I know it was hard working with this old soldier and I love you for it.

Our extended family who seem more like my brother and sister, Thomas and Peggy Graham, who had patience to put up with me when camping and fishing. Especially as their neighbor. Money can't buy this kind of friendship, only love and the Blessings from God can accomplish this.

Tracy Mayo, owner of the Douglas Enterprise newspaper, for her kind caring attitude and helping hand to an old country boy.

R.O. And Mary Mitchell, Evelyn Buchan and in memory of Mayor Derward Buchan who listened while I did the yapping during get togethers at Burger King over coffee and sandwiches.

ALSO FROM THOMASMAX PUBLISHING

Books by Fitzgerald's Paul B. Dunn

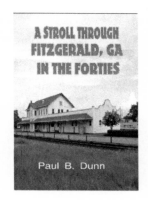

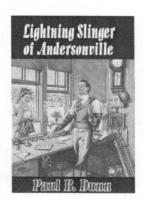

Fitzgerald's Paul B. Dunn offers three great books for South Georgia readers. *A Stroll Through Fitzgerald, GA, In The Forties* takes the reader on an imaginary but nostalgic tour through Paul's home town just after World War II, visiting real places and seeing real people. In addition, Paul has also penned biographies of his father, Teddie O'Dunn, in *Lightning Slinger of Andersonville*, and his mother, Anna, who earned the nickname of the book's title, *Tremble Chin*.

Each title is available for $14.95.

ThomasMax titles are available almost everywhere books are sold and through internet sellers such as Amazon.com. If your favorite bookstore doesn't have the title you want in stock, ask the store to order it for you. You may also order directly from the publisher's website at thomasmax.com. Payments at the publisher's website are processed via PayPal.

Lightning Source UK Ltd.
Milton Keynes UK
05 December 2009

147112UK00003B/4/P